MOON

52 THINGS TO DO IN

BOSTON

CAMERON SPERANCE

CONTENTS

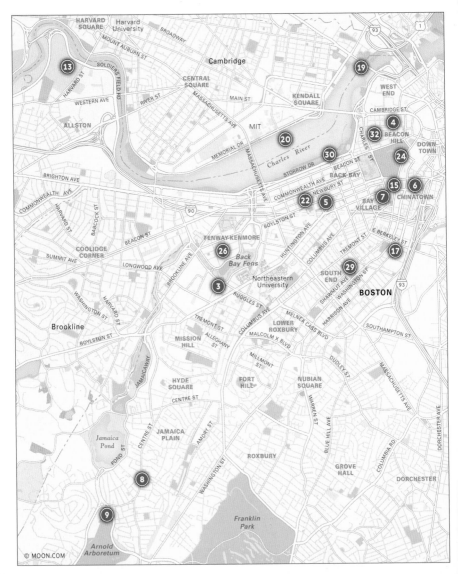

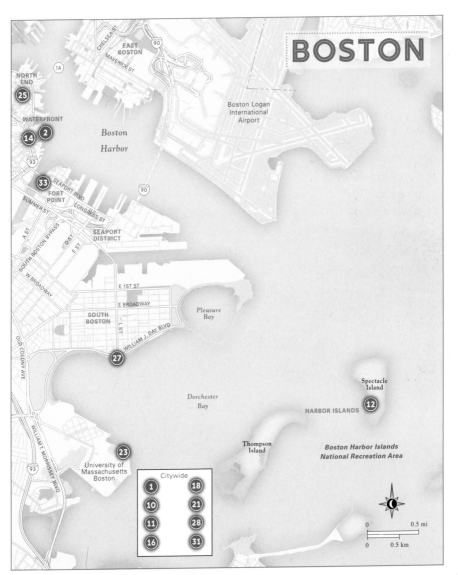

BOSTON

CHELSEA ST

EAST BOSTON

MAVERICK ST

1A

NORTH END

(25)

WATERFRONT

(14) (2)

93

Boston Logan International Airport

Boston Harbor

(33)

SEAPORT BLVD

FORT POINT

SUMMER ST

CONGRESS ST

A ST

D ST

90

SEAPORT DISTRICT

E ST

SOUTH BOSTON BYPASS

W BROADWAY

E 1ST ST

E BROADWAY

SOUTH BOSTON

I ST

WILLIAM J. DAY BLVD

Pleasure Bay

OLD COLONY AVE

(27)

Dorchester Bay

Spectacle Island

HARBOR ISLANDS

(12)

WILLIAM J. MORRISSEY BLVD

93

(23)

University of Massachusetts Boston

Thompson Island

Boston Harbor Islands National Recreation Area

Citywide

(1) (18)

(10) (21)

(11) (28)

(16) (31)

0   0.5 mi

0   0.5 km

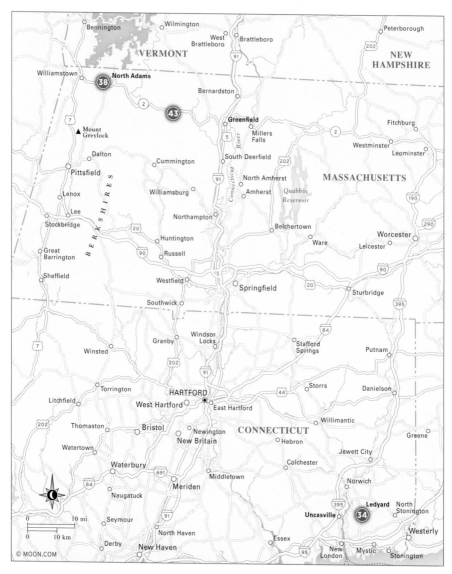

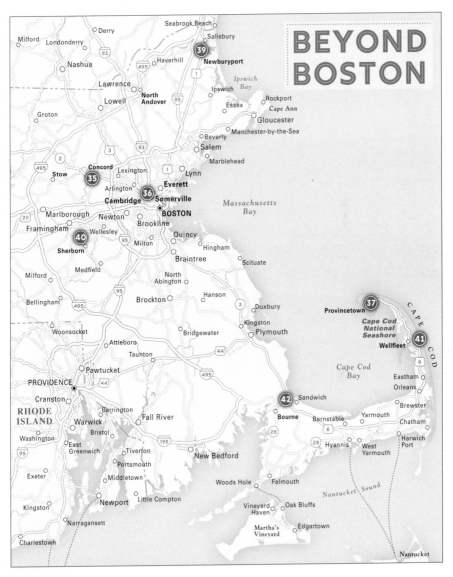

BEYOND BOSTON

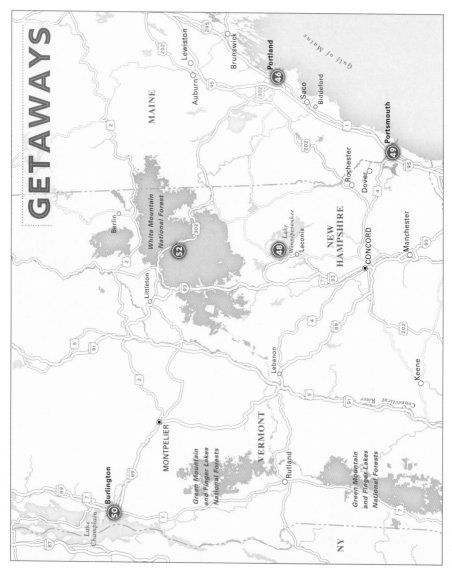

GETAWAYS

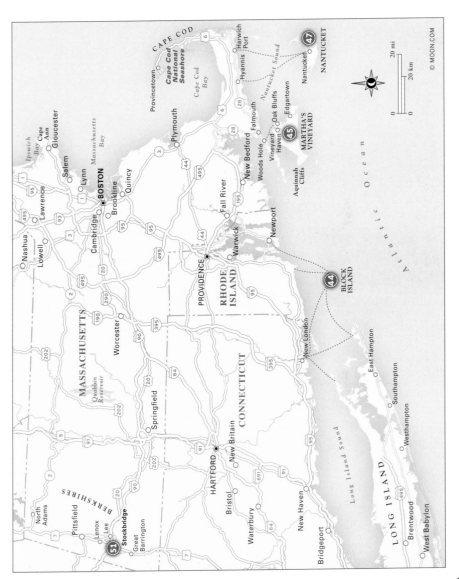

THIS IS BOSTON

What comes to mind when you think of Boston? Revolutionary War history. Paul Revere. Clam chowder and baked beans. Irish bars. Baseball. Ben Affleck and Matt Damon. Busy mornings and early nights. The curious way some of the people here really do pronounce "park" and "car" without the slightest hint of an "r" in there.

But there's more to Boston than all of that. Along the cobblestone streets you'll find hidden local gems like the lively Rose Kennedy Greenway, art galleries in the trendy South End, and eclectic shops and restaurants in Jamaica Plain.

On the Black Heritage Trail you'll learn about the impressive Abolitionists who called Boston home. In bustling food halls and cozy restaurants you'll enjoy some of the best cuisine in New England. Cheering for runners on Marathon Monday or just gawking at the architecture of Beacon Hill, you'll find friends for life. Sure, the Revolutionary War is woven throughout the city's past and present; Bostonians cherish their history—but the city is so much more than its past.

My favorite kind of Boston day starts with a run through South Boston into Seaport and Harborwalk, then a meet-up with a friend for coffee and a croissant from a South End bakery before wandering along Newbury Street and greeting the sunset with an early cocktail. If our favorite bands are in town, my husband and I will head to one of Boston's live music venues like the Sinclair—and all of that is just in one day.

One of the best things about Boston is its central location in New England, with a ton to explore in a relatively short distance. Spend weekends in places like the culturally rich Berkshires and LGBTQ+ proud Provincetown. Try your luck at a Connecticut casino, or hit the road for a fall foliage drive or an orchard. It's easy to get away from the hustle of city life and get a taste of something completely different. Even a quick daytrip to Walden Pond to channel your inner Thoreau can offer a dose of much-needed respite from a busy week.

Whether you're a born-and-bred Bostonian, a visitor, or this is where you're planting new roots, you'll find some of the best ways to understand the past and present that make the city iconic in this book.

▲ Boston Harbor

TO DO LISTS

Beantown Essential

1 Root for the **home team**

4 Walk the **Black Heritage Trail**

5 Marvel at the **Boston Public Library**

7 Soak in sequin overload at a **Jacques' drag show**

13 Rock out at the **Boston Calling Musical Festival**

18 Cheer on runners at the **Boston Marathon**

21 Taste-test **chowdah**

24 Customize the **Freedom Trail**

25 Eat **Italian food** on Hanover Street

Neighborhoods and City Streets

6 Feast in **Chinatown**

8 Explore quirky **Jamaica Plain**

17 Gallery hop in **SoWa**

22 Splurge on **Newbury Street**

25 Eat Italian food on **Hanover Street**

26 Explore **Fenway** beyond the Red Sox

29 Brunch around the World in the **South End**

32 Get to know the Boston Brahmin in **Back Bay** and **Beacon Hill**

Get Outside

9 Soak in nature at the **Arnold Arboretum**

14 Meander the **Rose Kennedy Greenway**

20 **Kayak** the Charles River

27 Soak up the sun on **Boston's Irish Riviera**

30 Stroll on the **Esplanade**

33 Play at **Martin's Park**

35 Get transcendental at **Walden Pond**

40 Go **apple-picking**

52 **Ski and hike** in the White Mountains

Drink and Dine

6 Feast in **Chinatown**

10 Go beyond Boston beer at a **local distillery**

11 **Whip up a meal** with professional chefs

16 Dine at a Boston **food hall**

21 Taste-test **chowdah**

25 Eat **Italian food** on Hanover Street

29 **Brunch** around the World in the South End

31 Go on a TV- and movie-themed **pub crawl**

41 Slurp **oysters** in Wellfleet

46 Taste **foodie paradise** in Portland, Maine

Fun for Families and Kids

2 Go **whale-watching** in Boston Harbor

3 Sleuth the **unsolved art heist** at the Isabella Stewart Gardner Museum

12 Escape to the **Boston Harbor Islands**

19 Geek out at the **Museum of Science**

23 Revisit **Kennedy's Camelot** at the John F. Kennedy Presidential Library and Museum

33 Play at **Martin's Park**

40 Go **apple-picking**

Architecture and Historic Spots

4 Walk the **Black Heritage Trail**

5 Marvel at the **Boston Public Library**

23 Revisit **Kennedy's Camelot** at the John F. Kennedy Presidential Library and Museum

24 Customize the **Freedom Trail**

35 Get transcendental at **Walden Pond**

36 Go beyond Harvard Yard in **Cambridge** and **Somerville**

43 Head East on the **Mohawk Trail**

On the Water

2 Go **whale-watching** in Boston Harbor

12 Escape to the **Boston Harbor Islands**

20 **Kayak** the Charles River

27 Soak up the sun on **Boston's Irish Riviera**

44 Get your feet wet at **New England's best beaches**

Art and Culture

3 Sleuth the **unsolved art heist** at the Isabella Stewart Gardner Museum

5 Marvel at the **Boston Public Library**

15 See **Broadway hits-to-be** in the Theater District

17 **Gallery hop** in SoWa

23 Revisit **Kennedy's Camelot** at the John F. Kennedy Presidential Library and Museum

38 Get inspired at **Mass MoCA**

Boston Parties

7 Soak in sequin overload at a **Jacques' drag show**

13 Rock out at the **Boston Calling Music Festival**

18 Cheer on runners at the **Boston Marathon**

28 Go to a **concert**

31 Go on a TV- and movie-themed **pub crawl**

34 Try your luck at **New England casinos**

37 **Celebrate Pride** in Provincetown

Day Trips

㉟ Get transcendental at **Walden Pond**

㊱ Go beyond Harvard Yard in **Cambridge** and **Somerville**

㊳ Get inspired at **Mass MoCA**

㊴ Find quintessential New England in **Newburyport**

㊵ Go **apple-picking**

㊶ Slurp oysters in **Wellfleet**

㊷ Cruise **Cape Cod** on Old King's Highway

㊸ Head East on the **Mohawk Trail**

㊽ Take in **fall foliage**

㊾ Shop local in **Portsmouth,** New Hampshire

Weekend Getaways

Boston

1 Root for the home team

Beantown Essential • Fun for Families and Kids

Why Go: Professional sporting events are always a good time, but Boston takes it to the next level thanks to a mix of history, storied rivalries, rambunctious fans, and iconic stadiums.

Where: Gillette Stadium, 1 Patriot Pl., Foxborough, 508/543-8200, www.gillettestadium.com • TD Garden, 100 Legends Wy., 617/624-1000, www.tdgarden.com • Fenway Park, 4 Jersey St., 877/733-7699, www.mlb.com/redsox/ballpark

Timing: Ideal times to take in one of the games depends on the respective team's season, but there is always at least one sport in season no matter the time of year.

It's hard to go far in a historically Catholic city like Boston without seeing a church, but there may be no cathedrals as sacred as the temples of Gillette Stadium, the TD Garden, and Fen-

▲ Fenway Park

way Park. This trio of professional sports venues are the holy places of Boston's other popular religions: the **Patriots,** the **Celtics,** the **Bruins,** and the **Red Sox.**

Boston has earned its nickname of "Titletown" due to an array of championship appearances and victories, with a string of World Series, Stanley Cup, NBA Finals, and Super Bowl wins in recent decades. The championship banners and trophies built one of the biggest sports fan bases in the U.S. while also creating a few, uh, jealous fans in other cities. And though Boston's title town reputation does ebb and flow with

legendary players like ex-Patriots quarterback Tom Brady coming and going, the city's status remains steadfast in the hearts of her fans.

Whether you've been in Boston all your life or are a transplant with stronger ties to certain teams down in New York City or elsewhere, hearing the roar of a crowd of die-hard fans while attending one of the local team's home games is a must-do experience.

A snowy December game at **Gillette Stadium** tests even the most loyal of Patriots fans (or maybe just their tolerance for cold weather), but they still show up in droves, ready to shout down Steelers and Giants fans in true Boston sports fandom style. The 65,000+ seat stadium was privately funded, and it was designed by HOK Sport who included artistic accents like a stylized lighthouse and seascape to showcase the region's coastal history. With a massive video board in the south end zone and thoughtful seat positioning (all of which point exactly toward midfield), there's no bad place to sit—which is good since the tickets aren't cheap ($60 to well over $1000, www.patriots.com/tickets). Concession stands offer everything from pizza to barbeque, brats to burritos. There's beer, too, of course. And, yes, everything is wildly overpriced. It's unfortunate that two beers and two hot dogs can easily run you $50, but that's about on par with most pro sports stadiums across the U.S.

The roar from **TD Garden,** whether in response to a slam dunk or a slap shot, is further proof of Boston's loyal fans. Known by locals as just "the Garden," the current arena is the second Boston Garden, this one having replaced the original in 1995. Home to both the NBA's

⌃ New England Patriots at Gillette Stadium

Celtics and the NHL's Bruins, the Garden is a multipurpose arena with over 19,000 seats. This ten-story building has everything you would expect from a sports arena: concession stands, executive suites, private restaurants, and a giant hi-def scoreboard. Perhaps the most notable element of the Garden is the parquet flooring of the basketball court. It's one of two arenas (the other being Orlando's Amway Center) to use parquet, which started due to high lumber costs following World War II but stuck around as a Boston legacy. Tickets to Celtics games are about $100, and Bruins tickets are around $150 (www.tdgarden.com/events/ticket-info). In addition to being a popular sports venue, the Garden has become more of a regional draw with the arrival of the adjoining Hub on Causeway development, which opened in late 2019. The development added office and apartment towers as well as better connections between the stadium and the North Station transit hub below. There are also sports bars, a food hall, and grocery store (no, you can't bring your own snacks inside to avoid sky-high concessions costs).

Summer games at **Fenway Park** are more than home runs and hot dogs—Neil Diamond's "Sweet Caroline" is an eighth-inning mainstay that turns the whole stadium into a singalong with 38,000 of your new best friends. Of all the sports temples in Boston, Fenway reigns supreme and it's the one that's been around the longest. First opened in 1912, Fenway has been renovated over the years to maintain its key presence in the local (and national) sports scene: it is the oldest active major league baseball stadium in the U.S. The 37-foot left field wall—dubbed the "Green Monster" after it was painted its namesake color in 1945—is one of the stadium's most iconic pieces of architecture. Its height prevents many homeruns from right-handed hitters, while giving those seated on top an incredible view of the entire park.

What you may not know is that Fenway Park got its name from the surrounding Fenway neighborhood rather than the other way around. The James E. McLaughlin-designed park was built to blend in with the neighborhood—a feat accomplished so well that former Red Sox pitcher Roger Clemens, upon his first visit in 1984, thought the taxi driver mistakenly dropped him off at a warehouse and not the stadium. You can expect standard ballpark fare like hot dogs, burgers, and sandwiches inside the stadium, but sports bars line the neighboring Lansdowne Street that runs the northern perimeter of Fenway. Tickets are a bit more reasonably priced, starting at $44 (https://www.mlb.com/redsox/tickets/single-game-tickets). You can also take a ballpark tour for $21.

The Curse of the Bambino

There are many local sports legends, but the most well-known belongs to the Red Sox and the Curse of the Bambino. After trading Babe Ruth to the New York Yankees in 1919, the Red Sox went until 2004 without winning a single World Series—a major blow to a team that won five of the first 15 championships. The Red Sox have since won several World Series, but local sports fans can't help but wonder if there are other sports curses around—especially after the Patriots and Tom Brady went their separate ways in 2020.

Traffic is always a nightmare, so use public transportation when you can. Fenway Park is near the Fenway and Kenmore Green Line stops, while the Garden is above North Station, which is served by both the Orange and Green Lines as well as commuter rail from northern suburbs. Gillette Stadium has an on-site commuter rail station with service to South Station downtown, but service is infrequent. Driving is your best bet to reach Gillette, but plan to sit in hours of traffic unless you leave early both ways.

Always wear gear from the home team, prepare to spend a lot of money if you're eating in the stadium, and plan to wait in long lines for restrooms. For winter games at Gillette, wear plenty of layers and use pocket and foot warmers to overcome the sometimes-unbearable chill. Be prepared to cheer until you're hoarse no matter what stadium you're in, and learn the lyrics to "Sweet Caroline" for Red Sox games—do Neil Diamond and Boston proud!

These sports venues may not have as much clout upstairs as the *actual* churches of Boston, but you would still be wise to follow a few commandments. Well, really just one: Thou shalt never support the Yankees.

Connect With...

26 Explore Fenway beyond the Red Sox

2 Go whale-watching
in Boston Harbor

Fun for Families and Kids • On the Water

Why Go: Not to sound too *Gilligan's Island,* but a "three-hour tour" is not only a great way to see some of the biggest marine life in New England, it's also an exciting way to get out on the water of Boston Harbor and beyond.

Where: The Boston Harbor Cruises terminal at Long Wharf in downtown • 877/733-9425, www.cityexperiences.com/boston/city-cruises/boston-harbor/whale-watch

Timing: Whale watches typically run from March through October each year.

Some of us may want to go on a whale-watching excursion because we think it's our chance to live out a Free Willy, whale-jumping-over-our-heads fantasy. Alas, the whale theatrics in these

▲ whale-watching tour

parts aren't quite up to Hollywood standards, but a whale-watching tour is still one of the few touristy things I repeatedly sign up for when friends or family are visiting from out of town.

The New England Aquarium partners with Boston Harbor Cruises from Long Wharf downtown, but this is a far cry from observing fish in tanks. It is an adventure to hop on a boat and head out into the Atlantic Ocean to see whales in their natural habitat. Half the fun is the anticipation of peering over the side of the boat and waiting for one of these huge, majestic sea creatures to crest above the water's surface.

The roughly three-to-four-hour tour heads into the Stellwagen Bank National Marine Sanctuary about an hour out of the harbor to the southeast. It's an enormous, 842-square-mile protected feeding area with an underwater plateau where deep-water currents churn up nutrients from hundreds of feet below. This attracts ocean mammals like whales and dolphins, as well as other marine life, including a variety of fish, and, yes, sharks.

You won't see any orcas (a la *Free Willy*), but there is often a mix of minkes, finbacks, and humpbacks visible here. New England Aquarium naturalists provide plenty of fun facts about

▲ breaching whale

the creatures who live in or pass through the sanctuary—and they do a great job preparing you for photo ops.

If for some reason you don't see a whale, tour operators will give you a free pass to return for another tour. However, I've gone on many of these trips and have always seen at least one or two pop up—though it sometimes takes all three or four hours to spot one. (Remember: they're mammals and still need fresh air, even if they're better underwater than any of us two-legged folks will ever be...save for Michael Phelps.)

While this is a kid-friendly activity, sharks do tend to come out in summer and early fall as seals move through the area. Jaws' relatives aren't going to jump onto the boat, but these finned predators may cause some vaguely disturbing seal-snacking gore in the water.

Plan ahead for your voyage: a windbreaker helps combat the sea breeze, occasional New England summer chill, and splashing waves. Seasickness medication is also useful for those with motion sickness. But no need pack food; most Boston Harbor Cruise vessels have a fully stocked bar and snack area with sandwiches and salads for sale.

Connect with . . .

🄰 Meander the Rose Kennedy Greenway
㉕ Eat Italian food on Hanover Street
㉝ Play at Martin's Park

Sleuth the unsolved art heist

at the Isabella Stewart Gardner Museum

Art and Culture • Fun for Families and Kids

Why Go: The Isabella Stewart Gardner Museum is both a beloved local cultural institution and a way to satisfy your hunger for a slice of unsolved true crime—all under one roof.

Where: The museum is on the eastern edge of the Fenway neighborhood, where the Longwood Medical Area meets the Emerald Necklace park network. The Museum of Fine Arts light rail station on the MBTA Green Line "E" branch is the most convenient public transportation. • 25 Evans Way, 617/566-1401, www.gardnermuseum.org

Timing: Even the gardens at the Isabella Stewart Gardner museum are indoors, so there is no bad time of year to pop in for a visit.

There are plenty of museums in town where you can gawk at beautiful paintings on the wall, but there is only one with a story as infamous as its masterpieces. In the early hours of March 18, 1990, thieves disguised as Boston Police officers gained entry into the museum, tied up the guards, and stole 13 works of art by master artists like Vermeer, Rembrandt, and Degas. In total, the art was worth $500 million, and the crime still ranks as the largest private property theft in the history of the world. The art is believed to have been offered for sale on the black market periodically since the theft; however, most leads have come up short and the case remains unsolved. Today, you'll see evidence of the incident in the gold frames left behind in the galleries, as well as enhanced museum security. Anyone able to provide information helping to return all 13 pieces to the museum in good condition will be rewarded with $10 million.

Docents throughout the museum are able to answer questions about the robbery as well as the entire remaining collection. Visitors can also rent a $5 audio guide, narrated by the museum's director of security, to retrace the steps of the intruders during their heist.

Of course, if you can't solve the mystery of the stolen paintings, there's still plenty of fun to be had at this house-turned-museum. Isabella Stewart Gardner, a Boston socialite who reigned over the city's culture scene from the late 1800s into the 1900s, bought the land in order to

▲ books at the museum

▲ sculptures in the courtyard

▲ Isabella Stewart Gardner Museum

build a Venetian-inspired home for the art she collected from around the world. The museum opened in 1903 and has served as one of the city's cultural hubs ever since. Three floors of art galleries fan off from a soaring courtyard with lush gardens. The soothing courtyard hosts a variety of events, including monthly cocktail parties that are intended to attract a younger crowd to visit and enjoy the museum.

The collection itself is quite varied, with more than 7,500 paintings from artists like Rembrandt and John Singer Sargent; roughly 7,000 artifacts from places like Ancient Rome, Renaissance Italy, Medieval Europe, Asia, and Islamic states; about 1,500 rare books; and a plethora of sculptures, silver, ceramics, and furniture. As you admire the collection, you'll notice there are limited description plaques around each work; Gardner preferred to let the art speak for itself.

You wouldn't be blamed for thinking the museum, with its mosaics and stonework in the courtyard coupled with a mix of centuries-old artwork in the galleries, was actually shipped over from Italy, but think again: this is a Boston original. You can thank Gardner's attention to detail for taking you on an Italian vacation in Massachusetts.

▲ the museum's courtyard and garden

Isabella Stewart Gardner: Socialite, Art Collector, and Red Sox Fan

They don't make socialites like Isabella Stewart Gardner anymore. A native New Yorker, Isabella Stewart made her way to Boston after marrying John Lowell Gardner. The couple's world tours inspired Isabella's fashion, bold personality, and enormous art collection. The art collecting led to her eponymous museum, but her personality is almost as bold as the art on the walls. Isabella once wore a Red Sox headband to a very formal performance of the Boston Symphony Orchestra—a major no-no in 1912! Along with the various ways to get a discount on museum admission, Isabella also left rules regarding the collection in her will. Should any of the art be rearranged from the way first established, the entire collection, as well as the entire museum property, is to be turned over to Harvard University. That puts even greater weight on the museum's "Look, don't touch" rule!

In addition to the museum's lighthearted attitude about the unsolved heist, you can also enjoy aspects of Gardner's fun-loving side. In celebration of her love for the Boston Red Sox, visitors in Red Sox apparel get discounted admission (an easy enough task for a local!). Guests named Isabella or those visiting on their birthday get free admission—be sure to bring your ID!

Connect With...

16 Dine at a Boston food hall
26 Explore Fenway beyond the Red Sox

4 **Walk the Black Heritage Trail**

Beantown Essential • Architecture and Historic Spots

Why Go: The important Black Heritage Trail gives visitors insight into the role of Boston's Black residents in the Abolitionist Movement leading up to and after the Civil War.

Where: The signed trail starts a few blocks behind the Massachusetts State House and covers much of the "North Slope" of Beacon Hill.

Timing: Self-guided tours of the trail are possible at all times of the year, with maps available at landmarks like the Abiel Smith School. If you prefer a guided tour, the National Park Service offers free 90-minute tours that start from the Robert Gould Shaw and 54th Regiment Memorial. These guided tours are operated in partnership with the nearby Museum of African American History and take place in spring, summer, and fall.

Most visitors and Boston locals have walked the Freedom Trail, but not everyone realizes there is a similar historic trail through the heart of the city, marking key landmarks in Black history.

Robert Gould Shaw and 54th Regiment Monument

The 1.6-mile Black Heritage Trail winds through Beacon Hill, connecting 15 sites associated with the Black community who fought for equal rights and emancipation leading up to, during, and after the Civil War.

Enslaved Africans were brought to Boston in 1638, but the American Revolution, during which many enslaved people fought on behalf of the colonies, was a turning point for the Abolitionist Movement in Massachusetts. After the war, the movement accelerated thanks to the determined efforts of the free African American community in Boston, and in 1790, Massachusetts became the only U.S. state to have no record of enslaved people during the first national census.

Between 1800 and 1900, most Black people who lived in Boston resided in what was known as the North Slope of Beacon Hill, which is where the Black Heritage Trail begins.

If you opt for the self-guided tour, start your walk at 46 Joy Street, about two minutes

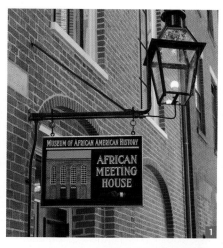

1: The Museum of African American History
2: Lewis and Harriet Hayden House **3:** African
Meeting House **4:** interior of The Museum of
African American History

northwest of the Massachusetts State House. This official start of the trail, formerly the **Abiel Smith School,** is now home to the **Museum of African American History** (46 Joy St., 617/725-0022, www.maah.org, $10 admission). But it began as the first building in the U.S. purposely built for educating Black children. It was named for Abiel Smith, who left a $4,000 endowment to the city for such an educational purpose. The school finally closed in 1855 after Black children were allowed to attend whatever school was closest to their own homes instead.

Behind the schoolhouse (and also part of the museum) is the **African Meeting House** (8 Smith Ct.), nicknamed the Black Faneuil Hall for its reputation for community organizing and hosting many great speeches during the Abolitionist Movement. Frederick Douglass spoke here in 1860, passionately expressing the need for free speech. In 1863, the meeting house became the site where African American soldiers volunteered to fight in the 54th Massachusetts Infantry Regiment lead by Colonel Robert Gould Shaw.

The next three stops were homes of Black residents during the 19th century. (Note: all the residences on the trail are currently inhabited by private citizens, so you cannot go inside.) Just across the narrow alley from the African Meeting House are the six wood-paneled **Smith Court Residences.** Farther along the trail on Phillips Street are **John Coburn House** (2 Phillips St.) and **Lewis and Harriet Hayden House** (66 Phillips St.). John Coburn House was home to John Coburn, a local businessman who was also the treasurer of the New England Freedom Association, which provided help to enslaved people seeking freedom. The Lewis and Harriett Hayden House was home to Black abolitionists Lewis and Harriet Hayden, who escaped enslavement in Kentucky. Their home was a key "station" on the Underground Railroad network enslaved people used to escape from the South to freedom. The Haydens were also consulted by Harriett Beecher Stowe when she wrote Uncle Tom's Cabin.

After the Hayden house, head west to Charles Street, the main commercial thoroughfare running through the neighborhood. **The Charles Street Meeting House** (70 Charles St.), a towering red-brick building, was originally built as a church, later becoming the first integrated church in Boston before transitioning to a meeting house. Over the years, it has served as a safe haven for abolitionists, suffragettes, and the LGBTQ+ community.

Northeast of the Charles Street Meeting House is the **John J. Smith House** (86 Pinckney St.). John J. Smith owned a barbershop, which was a safe meeting place for abolitionists helping enslaved people along the Underground Railroad. Smith also served in the Civil War and was elected to the House of Representatives for three terms.

Continue east from John J. Smith House on Pinckney Street until you reach the intersection of Pinckney and Anderson. On the corner stands the beautiful **Phillips School** (65 Anderson St.), which became one of the first integrated schools in Boston in 1855 due to the tireless efforts of the Black community.

Farther down Pinckney Street is **George Middleton House** (5 Pinckney St.). Erected in 1797, this is the oldest existing, Black-built home on Beacon Hill. Owner George Middleton was a Revolutionary War veteran who led the all-Black "Bucks of America" militia in the war. Middleton was also a founder of the African Society, which helped lay the groundwork for the 19th-century Abolitionist Movement.

From George Middleton House, head south on Joy Street and then east on Beacon Street to reach the bronze **Robert Gould Shaw and 54th Regiment Memorial** (across from the State House at 24 Beacon St.), sculpted by Augustus Saint-Gaudens. The sculpture honors the African American volunteer infantry from the Revolutionary War, as well as its leader, mentioned earlier, Robert Gould Shaw. The regiment was made famous for its assault on Fort Wagner in an effort to capture the city of Charleston, South Carolina. While the regiment suffered a large loss of life (including Shaw's) in the battle, their defeat inspired more Black soldiers to enlist in the army to help the Union.

Once you've reached the memorial, you're at the end of the Black Heritage Trail, mere steps away from the busy Park Street and Downtown Crossing subway stations for convenient transportation to your next destination.

Connect With...
30 Stroll on the Esplanade

Marvel at the Boston Public Library

Architecture and Historic Spots • Beantown Essential • Art and Culture

Why Go: The ornate, Parisian and Italian-inspired design of the Boston Public Library's McKim Building is one of the most iconic pieces of architecture in the entire city—and that's just the beginning. The impressive collections within, including gorgeous artwork and rare manuscripts, lend credence to historic claims by William Tudor that Boston may be the Athens of America.

Where: Located in the heart of Copley Square in Boston's Back Bay neighborhood, the McKim Building is easily accessed via the Copley station on the MBTA Green Line subway, which stops on the same block as the library • 230 Dartmouth St., 617/536-5400, www.bpl.org

Timing: The McKim Building is accessible all year long, but visitors may find portions of the library closed off during peak wedding season in the summer.

You might think the bookish quiet of a library isn't as thrilling as a day out on the town, but the grand presence of the main branch of the Boston Public Library system in the heart of Boston's urban core is enough to make anyone excited about libraries.

▲ Boston Public Library

The Boston Public Library's McKim Building faces the Trinity Church and 200 Clarendon St., Boston's tallest skyscraper, across Copley Square. Architecture buffs may argue about which building made a more significant contribution to the city's architectural design reputation, but the McKim Building—named for its architect Charles Follen McKim—will always be my personal favorite. Inspired by the Sainte-Geneviève Library in Paris, the McKim was declared a "palace for the people" when it opened in 1895. As a reminder of just how egalitarian this palatial house of learning is, a carving of Minerva, the Roman goddess of wisdom, flanks the main entrance with the library's motto, "Free to All," carved into the building.

Start your tour of the building from the outside. The Renaissance and Beaux-Arts architecture can make this people's palace seem a little intimidating at first glance, but upon further

the Roman-inspired courtyard

Bates Hall

marble lions at the Boston Public Library

inspection, you can see the architect's charming care for detail. The copper molding around the terra-cotta roof features alternating dolphin and seashell designs, paying homage to Boston's deep maritime history. Just above the Minerva carving over the front door, you'll find three seals representing the City of Boston, Commonwealth of Massachusetts, and the library itself. The final pieces of exterior artwork are the statues of women on either side of the main entrance on Dartmouth Street. These are actually allegorical statues by sculptor Bela Pratt, representing art (the one holding a paint palette and brush) and science (the one holding a globe). You're learning so much, and you haven't even set foot in the library yet!

Head into the vestibule but stop before making your way into the lobby. You'll see three Daniel Chester French-sculpted bronze doors with different allegorical figures: truth, romance, knowledge, wisdom, music, and poetry. When you're ready, head inside.

The pink marble walls, Italian mosaic floors, and vaulted ceilings of the lobby seem a little more like Versailles than a quiet place to study (I promise you there are reading rooms here, too). The lobby owes its pink wall hues to Tennessee marble—a building material also featured at Grand Central Terminal in New York City and the United States Capitol. Spanish builder Rafael Gustavino is responsible for the vaulted ceilings, which have a tiled, vine pattern throughout the main entryway.

The pink tones eventually give way to an ivory gray limestone grand staircase that is embedded with fossil shells. The walls here are made from yellow Siena marble; pay close attention—McKim is said to have reviewed 10 times the amount of marble actually needed to find the perfect pieces, so take a minute to soak it all in.

A pair of marble lions, sculpted by Louis Saint-Gaudens, are included in the staircase and were added in memory of the Massachusetts Second and Twentieth volunteer infantries in the U.S. Civil War. The lions were delivered unpolished as a result of a time crunch to open the library on time. While there was a debate over whether to ever polish them (surviving members of the infantries thought the unpolished look had greater meaning), visitors to the library since its opening in 1895 have rubbed the sculptures' tails for good luck, revealing the yellow marble beneath in the process.

As the staircase sweeps visitors from the main entrance up to the second floor, the impressive Pierre Puvis de Chavannes murals become visible. The eight panels portray figures representing different disciplines visitors can seek out in the library's archives, including history, philosophy, sciences, and various types of poetry. As you admire the murals, continue up the stairs and you'll eventually stumble into **Bates Hall**—the library's most ornate reading room—with 50-foot arched ceilings and rows of desks where visitors can study, read, or finish up a deadline under green-shaded lamps. (Note: Not that it's ever a good idea to chat in a library, but this is definitely a room where they're serious about that "no talking" rule!)

Other attractions within the McKim Building include the **John Singer Sargent gallery** on the third floor, which includes his *Triumph of Religion* murals, depicting various religious stories and iconography from belief systems around the world. **The Abbey Room,** just off Bates Hall, is also worth a stop. Previously referred to as the "Book Delivery Room," the Abbey Room is home to beautiful murals by *Harper's Magazine* illustrator Edwin Austin Abbey, depicting the quest for the holy grail. For those wanting to enjoy the library outside the quiet zones, stroll around the **Roman-inspired courtyard** at the center of the building. This open-air plaza, with gardens and a fountain, is a great spot to unwind with a snack from the café while soaking in the library's gilded glory.

Of course, as a branch of the Boston Public Library, the McKim Building is also home to countless books—including priceless rare ones. The collection spans roughly 4,000 years and includes everything from cuneiform tablets to early works of William Shakespeare.

Connect With...

22 Splurge on Newbury Street

30 Stroll on the Esplanade

32 Get to know the Boston Brahmin in Back Bay and Beacon Hill

Feast in Chinatown

Neighborhoods and City Streets • Drink and Dine

Why Go: Chinatown offers a genuine taste of Asian cuisines, from spicy Szechuan to sweet custard tarts. Here you'll find a mix of dumplings, Peking duck (if you order in advance), hot pot, and other scrumptious dishes up and down Beach Street and in the surrounding area.

Where: Chinatown is just south of downtown Boston and is best accessed from the Chinatown Orange Line subway station.

Timing: There isn't a bad time to visit Chinatown—and some of the only restaurants in Boston open past 10pm are found in this neighborhood. It's the city's prime spot for a late-night bite.

Walk under the Chinatown Gate on Beach Street and you'll find yourself in a bustling enclave of noodle shops, bakeries, and dim sum dining rooms that bring in a diverse mix of patrons from across the city. The neon-lit streets can be overwhelming for first-time visitors wanting to enjoy the neighborhood's delicious (and seemingly never-ending) kitchens but unsure of where to start. Have no fear: I've made a list of my favorite spots.

▲ red-bean-filled Moon Cakes

Show up with an empty stomach to take full advantage of the many dim sum carts getting pushed through the expansive dining room at **China Pearl** (9 Tyler St., 617/426-4338, www.chinapearlboston.com), easily noticeable from the street by its yellow sign out front. This lovely restaurant holds a special place in my heart; it was where I tasted dim sum for the first time, and the staff couldn't have been nicer explaining the variety of steamed buns and other options available. Enjoy classics like General Gau's Chicken, dumplings, and lo meins.

If you're longing for a hands-on cooking/dining combo experience, follow Harrison Avenue to **Kaze Shabu Shabu** (1 Harrison Ave., 617/338-8283, www.kazeshabushabuma.com),

▲ China Pearl

▲ bao

▲ Shōjō

the neighborhood hub for hot pot with a variety of broths, noodles, and enough meats and fish to feed as many guests as you can fit around the in-table cooking setup. They also have tasty vegetarian options and great cocktails—try one of the refreshing smoothies.

The red marquee of **Empire Garden** (690 Washington St., 617/482-8898) makes it easy to spot the restaurant, which serves up a wide array of classic (and sometimes Americanized) Chinese cuisine. Originally the Globe Theater, hosting vaudeville acts in the early 1900s, Empire Garden occupies what was the theater's beautiful mezzanine level. The kitchen offers a steady stream of dim sum carts packed with dumplings and sesame buns, as well as Peking duck (call ahead and order at least one hour before arrival).

Glitzier-minded diners will favor **Shōjō** (9 Tyler St., 617/482-8887, www.shojoboston.com), a street art-clad Asian fusion gastropub with impeccable cocktails and just-as-impeccable bar bites. Try creative drinks like the Mai Tai Hobnob (made with Thai chili-infused tequila) or the Morning Star (with mezcal, elderflower liquor, and Crème de Pamplemousse), or choose from their great list of sakes and beers. Their food menu is full of delicious, creative options like smoked barbeque pork bao, fried lemongrass and chicken dumplings, kimchi fried rice, and mushroom mazemen.

Peach Farm (4 Tyler St., 617/482-1116, www.peachfarmseafood.com), another favorite of mine just across the street from Shōjō, is majorly popular with restaurant industry workers and famished crowds pouring out of nearby Theater District nightclubs. The typical 3am closing time here gives night owls the opportunity to feast on an extensive menu of unique seafood dishes like lobster with ginger and scallions, clams in black bean sauce, and spicy dry-fried salted squid. There are also more takeout-style Chinese options like chicken and rice dishes, and—unlike other restaurants in the neighborhood—the Peking duck doesn't need to be ordered well ahead of arrival.

No matter where you go for dinner, be sure to save room for the sweet treats at **Great Taste Bakery & Restaurant** (63 Beach St., 617/426-8899, www.greattastebakery.com). Panda-shaped cakes, Portuguese egg tarts, and custards are just a fraction of the items you'll find in the bakery case. Grab a box of your favorites, and (maybe) a few will remain by the time you get home.

Don't bother driving for this food pilgrimage; parking is a nightmare. Take advantage of

Origins: Boston's Chinatown

Boston's Chinatown neighborhood is one of the largest of its kind outside New York City. The area's Chinese roots date as far back as 1870, and immigration grew in the mid-1900s following the abolition of the Chinese Exclusion Act, which had banned Chinese immigration into the U.S. from 1882 to 1943.

Chinatown went through some grittier years when its western border was known as the Combat Zone, a city-designated adult entertainment district. Neighborhood residents formed a grassroots initiative to bring down crime in the area, which eventually led to the shuttering of most of the seedier venues in the neighborhood. By the time of the Big Dig in the 1990s and into the early 2000s, Chinatown had built a new reputation as a bustling restaurant row.

Chinatown's easy access to public transit via the T. If you have time after enjoying a delicious meal (or two), stroll along the streets and soak in the atmosphere.

Connect With...

🄔 Meander the Rose Kennedy Greenway
🄗 Gallery Hop in SoWA

7

Soak in sequin overload at a Jacques' drag show

Beantown Essential • Boston Parties

Why Go: Drag shows are a reigning source of LGBTQ+ pride, showcasing the camp and freedom this community both treasures and continues to fight for.

Where: Jacques' Cabaret, 79 Broadway St., 617/426-8902, www.jacques-cabaret.com

Timing: Friday and Saturday nights are typically the rowdiest times of the week to see a show, no matter the time of year.

Tucked down a side street of townhouses in the shadows of some of Boston's flashiest residential and office real estate lies a surviving bit of Boston's oldest LGBTQ+ commercial identity. At a time when so many bars and nightclubs of its kind have shuttered, Jacques' Cabaret lumbers on in all its tasseled, lace front, high-heeled glory.

Gay bars used to be more prevalent in Boston and even fanned across multiple neighborhoods, from Bay Village to the Back Bay and Beacon Hill over to the Fenway. But as the LGBTQ+ community became more accepted by the rest of the city, and with the rise of "dating" apps like Grindr, many bar patrons felt it unnecessary to gather solely in these spaces. Major venues like Buddie's in Back Bay, Sporter's in Beacon Hill, and Machine in the Fenway have come and gone—but Jacques' remains a staple.

When you hear muffled (albeit still blaring) music through a black security door beneath a red awning, you've reached Jacques' Cabaret. Walk in, and you'll immediately notice how dark this small space is. The black walls, faded posters, and dim lights perfectly set the tone and make it clear right away: all eyes should be on the queens performing on the main stage and nowhere else.

The first rule of Jacques' is bring cash—a lot of it. The bar is cash only, and paper bills are the currency of choice for drag performers. (These queens need to pay the rent just like anyone else!) The second rule is no judgment. Jacques' has turned into a bit of a cornucopia of Boston. Bachelorette parties are now the largest source of clients, but this raucous night out is still a

1: Candace Persuasion working the crowd
2: a stage performance **3:** Kris Knievel (center) is the main attraction at Jacques'. **4:** performer Dee Dee de Ray

favorite among members of the LGBTQ+ community (yours truly included), and it is still very much a safe space for LGBTQ+ people. Visitors should remember that and remain respectful of the original supportive community of the bar (there aren't that many spaces like it left in Boston.) Political commentary and messages of love undercoat all that searing sass and sequined glamour that goes into a drag performance.

Names like Destiny, Mizery, and Kris Knievil grace the main stage with lip-synched, raunchy performances that rip through the crowd, often involving audience participation and objectifying any males that appear to have remotely flat stomachs. Drinks err on the expensive side for their size, but they are also potent (likely in an effort to encourage clientele to generously tip the talent). As far as dress code goes, don't feel the need to put on your finest attire, and I wouldn't recommend dressing up in drag yourself—unless you're auditioning, that is—but wearing a boa or two isn't out of the question.

Is it *RuPaul's Drag Race* competition-caliber choreography? Absolutely not. But after a few $10 thimbles of vodka sodas that seem to always skip the soda part of the equation, the per-

▲ performers at Jacques'

Safe Havens

Like in many cities, the bulk of Boston's brick-and-mortar LGBTQ+ institutions have faded away. But there are still a few surviving gay bars, and it's important to protect them! These spaces played an important role in LGBTQ+ history, as havens where members of the community would rally in the ongoing fight for equal rights and protection. At a time when politicians across the country chip away at rights for Transgender people and other members of the community, the need for spaces like this is definitely not diminishing.

formers here will start to resemble drag stars like Bianca del Rio, Naomi Smalls, or Lady Bunny. Given Jacques' typically early last call, after the show you'll even have enough time to walk up a few blocks to enjoy some songs at Club Café, Boston's hub of LGBTQ+ nightlife.

Connect With...

🔟 Gallery hop in SoWA
㉙ Brunch around the World in the South End

Explore quirky Jamaica Plain

Neighborhoods and City Streets • Drink and Dine

Why Go: Most people head to Jamaica Plain to visit the Samuel Adams Boston Brewery, but Boston's most famous brewery is just one of the cool stops in this beautiful, diverse, and quirky neighborhood.

Where: Jamaica Plain is southwest of downtown Boston on the Orange Line subway of the MBTA. The most convenient stops are the Green and Forest Hills stations.

Timing: There's really no bad time of year to do things like visit the Samuel Adams Brewery, but exploring the neighborhood is certainly a more enjoyable experience if you venture out in late spring, summer, or early fall. Winter months are good for popping into a cozy restaurant on Centre Street.

Not quite the suburbs, nor a buzzy city downtown, Jamaica Plain (or JP, as it's known to locals) is one of the most progressive and diverse parts of Boston—and one of the most naturally picturesque; its extensive farmland earned JP the title "Eden of America" in newspapers in the 1800s. Today, you'll see the sprawling farms have been replaced with Centre Street's (JP's main drag) organic-minded restaurants, fair trade coffee shops, specialty boutiques, and thrift shops.

Right in the middle of bustling Centre Street, and representative of some of the admirable values of JP, is **Boomerangs** (716 Centre St., 617/524-5120, www.shopboomerangs.org), a popular thrift shop that provides funding to the AIDS Action HIV prevention and wellness group. Pop in for handmade clothing, a variety of books, and unique jewelry. Down the street is **City Feed and Supply** (672 Centre St., 617/524-1700, www.cityfeedandsupply.com), part grocery store and part deli. Try the Italian sandwich or vegan BLT.

South of Boomerangs and City Feed is the women-led bookstore **Papercuts** (60 South St., 617/522-3404, www.papercutsjp.com). This award-winning local favorite feels more like someone's hip apartment than a typical bookstore, thanks to owner Kate Layte. Check out the curated reading lists or simply browse the bright shop to find your next great read.

Don't skip **Salmagundi** (765 Centre St., 617/522-5047, www.salmagundiboston.com),

the hat emporium. Even if you don't think you look good in hats, stop here. At least one of the thousands of bowlers, wide brim, cloche, or other options on the shelves will appeal to your inner fashion icon and give you the positive hat-wearing experience you never knew you needed.

For the perfect bridge between shopping and dining, head to **Tres Gatos** (470 Centre St., 617/477-4851, www.tresgatosjp.com). Originally a book and music store, the space was reinvented as a tapas restaurant but held onto the book and record retail. Tres Gatos was founded on a principle that shouldn't be too hard for any of us to abide by: "good food, music, and books are essential to a happy life." I'm always happy with a good tune and a book, but the chickpea fritters and lamb bocadillo from Tres Gatos lead me to even greater happiness!

Another spot for a tasty bite is **Ten Tables** (597 Centre St., 617/524-8810, www.tentables. net), a small (yes, there are only ten tables) restaurant in the heart of JP that serves up scrumptious fare like saffron risotto with braised lamb or seared scallops with chorizo and crispy chickpeas.

Samuel Adams Boston Brewery

Taste Samuel Adams's brews.

Jamaica Pond

Origins: Jamaica Plain

Jamaica Plain is removed enough from Boston's urban core that it was largely farmland, summer homes, and estates from the pre-Revolutionary War era through the mid-1800s. JP's claim to fame is being one of America's first streetcar suburbs, connected to downtown Boston with trolley service. But Boston eventually absorbed JP into city limits, and the neighborhood boomed in population with the arrival of the city's "triple decker," a three-story apartment house where members of the same extended family often occupied all three floors.

The arrival of German immigrants into the neighborhood as well as access to a local aquifer appealed to brewers. Highland Spring Brewery, Haffenreffer Brewery, and the American Brewing Company were among the first—until Prohibition. But Boston Brewing Company, owner of Samuel Adams, is the longest-lasting beer legacy of JP.

Of course, you won't want to miss the **Samuel Adams Boston Brewery** (30 Germania St., 617/368-5080, www.samueladams.com). This neighborhood institution was one of the country's first craft breweries, and it's still cranking out national treasures like the Boston Lager. (It's also the official beer of Fenway Park.) See how the tasty brews are made on a fun and informative brewery tour (every half hour, suggested $2 donation), complete with pitchers of refreshing Sam Adams beers to taste.

When the weather's nice, visit the shores of **Jamaica Pond** for an afternoon of reading and relaxing, or wander the pond-side trail. You can also rent boats for sailing through **Courageous Sailing** (www.couragoussailing.org).

No matter how you spend your time in JP, you'll enjoy getting to know this friendly, community-minded neighborhood.

Connect With...

❸ Sleuth the unsolved art heist at the Isabella Stewart Gardner Museum
❾ Soak in nature at the Arnold Arboretum

Soak in nature at the Arnold Arboretum

Get Outside • Fun for Families and Kids

Why Go: The Arnold Arboretum of Harvard University is the oldest public arboretum in North America—and a truly beautiful place to learn about plants.

Where: The Arnold Arboretum in Boston's Jamaica Plain neighborhood is about 20 minutes southwest, driving from Boston's Back Bay neighborhood. If using public transportation, it takes about a half hour to ride the Orange Line to the Forest Hills terminus and then walk about 15 minutes • 125 Arborway, 617/524-1718, www. arboretum.harvard.edu

Timing: The Arnold Arboretum is open every day of the year, but there are better times to visit than others. Summer and fall are my favorite times to go, as plants and flowers are in bloom and colors are at their most vibrant.

Sure, there are plenty of parks closer to downtown Boston where you can easily have a picnic with friends or relax with a good book for a few hours. But the 281-acre Arnold Arboretum is so much more than just a neighborhood park.

▲ Hunnewell Building

Harvard came into control of the Arnold Arboretum in the 1800s after whaling merchant James Arnold left a portion of his estate to the university with the wish that it go toward promoting agriculture and horticulture. Arnold's gift was paired with a country estate to form the Arnold Arboretum. A thousand-year lease struck between the City of Boston and Harvard means the city maintains the perimeter of the park and, in turn, Harvard keeps the grounds open daily to the public, free of charge.

Landscape architect Frederick Law Olmsted was commissioned to design the botanical space, and he included it as a link in his Emerald Necklace of parks spanning from Jamaica Plain to Downtown Crossing. Olmsted and the arboretum's first curator, Charles Sprague Sargent, mapped out the arboretum to group plants and trees by family and so

autumn at the arboretum

Arnold Arboretum

path through the arboretum

that "a visitor driving through the Arboretum will be able to obtain a general idea of the arborescent vegetation of the north temperate zone without even leaving his carriage."

The arboretum amassed its collection of global flora through expeditions, particularly to eastern Asia and throughout the United States. Many of those plants with roots (pardon the pun) dating back to the 1870s still grow in the arboretum today. Magnolias, lilacs, gingko, and bonsai are just a few of the species in this beautiful, extensive collection.

When you arrive at the arboretum, you'll encounter the brick Hunnewell Building, a visitors center named for railroad financier and botanist H.H. Hunnewell, at the main gate. Drop in to get a map and up-to-date information on the collection. You can also set up a free guided tour with one of the docents on-site. These tours offer a more in-depth look at everything from fall fruits to azaleas as well as other features of the arboretum and its more than 16,000 plants.

If you prefer the self-guided experience, the arboretum also offers its Expeditions mobile app, which provides information on the plant collection and history from the convenience of your smartphone, allowing you to explore at your own pace.

▲ spring at the Arnold Arboretum

Another fun way to learn more about the arboretum's extensive collection is by joining the Tree Mobs, 30-minute meetings with scientists at various spots in the park, providing more information on a select part of the collection. Experts are on hand to share fun facts, the history of how the plant or accompanying wildlife came into the collection, and why it is so important to the surrounding region. A past Tree Mob included attendees going out with flashlights on an early evening in winter to observe Great Horned Owls ahead of their nesting season. The schedule and locations of these gatherings are posted on the arboretum's website.

The most picturesque spot in the arboretum is Peters Hill, the tallest of the four hills found within the arboretum's grounds. You'll see runners and those walking at a more leisurely pace all heading to Peters peak to get a great view of the Boston skyline to the east. Take a few hours for yourself to leave the city stress behind and enjoy a botany-fueled afternoon with a view.

Connect With...

8 Explore quirky Jamaica Plain

10 Go beyond Boston beer at a local distillery

Drink and Dine

Why Go: Boston's known for its great craft beer, but the city's distilleries could give the beer scene a run for its money.

Where: Bully Boy Distillers, 44 Cedric St., 617/442-6000, www.bullyboydistillers.com • Boston Harbor Distillery, 12R Ericsson St., 617/533-7001, www.shop.bostonharbordistillery.com • GrandTen Distilling, 383 Dorchester Ave., 617/269-0497, www.grandten.com

Timing: These distilleries are open year-round, but given their speakeasy vibes, it's better to go in colder months. Why waste a nice summer day in a dark bar? OK, fine. Summer months are good, too.

Boston is known for its numerous craft breweries, from Samuel Adams in Jamaica Plain to Harpoon in the Seaport. But sometimes...you just need a stiff drink. Luckily, Boston has a flair for the hard stuff, too. Local distilleries aren't as prevalent as breweries, but they still have a cult following for their creative cocktails, activities, and tours.

If you're a distillery novice, don't feel intimidated; the talented mixologists can help you order a drink that fits your tastes. And feel free to watch them artfully prepare your cocktails—that's half the fun! Also, don't forget to bring cash so you can tip the mixologists for their skills and attention to detail.

Bully Boy Distillers in Boston's Newmarket industrial neighborhood, labeled itself as the city's first craft distillery. That may or may not be true, but it's certainly the most popular, thanks to its range of house-made spirits (which fans can also purchase at most liquor stores in the area), fresh juices, and seasonal ingredients. Bully Boy's headquarters isn't exactly pristine, as it's basically in the heart of a warehouse hub, but a walk into the dark tasting room feels akin to stepping into a Prohibition speakeasy. The velvet booths, dark walls, and expansive bar are enough to make you lose track of time—a few negronis or a flight of old-fashioned cocktails help with that, too. Bully Boy is known for its white whiskey (yes, that's a thing), so don't miss out on the smoky, grapefruit-tinged Flower and Flame.

▲ Boston Harbor Distillery

▲ inside Boston Harbor Distillery

Be sure to take a production room tour ($10), where the team not only shows visitors around, but also doles out tips on how to make your best at-home cocktails. The tour lasts about an hour and ends in the tasting room, where cocktails run between $12 and $14; an old-fashioned flight costs $18.

A little off the beaten path to the south is **Boston Harbor Distillery** in Dorchester. Housed in a 19th century waterfront warehouse, this distillery offers a tasting room and beautiful lounge space for its visitors. Try New England Harvest, made with Putnam Rye, cranberry juice, lemon juice, and maple syrup. If you like what you taste, you can purchase their wide range of house-made spirits on-site. Boston Harbor also offers two different tour options: the 1.5-hour VIP whiskey tour and tasting ($50) and the 30-minute distillery sampler ($20).

South Boston's **GrandTen Distilling** houses its production of small-batch spirits in what was at one time the nation's largest iron foundry that produced ammunition for the War of 1812. Since 2012, GrandTen has been producing acclaimed libations, such as its Wire Works Gin, the Fire Puncher Vodka, and South Boston Irish Whiskey. Weekends are the best time

▲ whiskey flight

Mr. Boston

Boston's last great turn with distilleries came during the "Mr. Boston" era of the 1900s. Mr. Boston was a distillery on Massachusetts Avenue just blocks from where Bully Boy Distillers now stands. The Mr. Boston distillery, which began in 1933 and ran through the 1980s, produced bourbon, rum, and brandy. But its best-known brand was the *Mr. Boston Official Bartender's Guide*, a craft cocktail book known as the "Bible of Booze." While the distillery has shuttered, you can still access the guide in digital form at www. mrbostondrinks.com.

to visit, as you can reserve a spot at the Friday Night Flights tasting event (starting at $20) each week, which includes a detailed tour followed by a tasting of the full lineup of products. Free tours take place each Saturday afternoon during open tasting room hours. GrandTen also serves small bar bites and lets guests bring in takeout from other restaurants.

Is Boston ever going to suddenly choose whiskey over a brewski? No. But is this trio enough to make you go local with your whiskey when you're ordering a Manhattan at a bar? Absolutely.

Connect With...

17 Gallery hop in SoWA

23 Revisit Kennedy's Camelot at the John F. Kennedy Presidential Library and Museum

11 Whip up a meal with professional chefs

Drink and Dine

Why Go: You can have a fancy meal out on the town any time, but learning how your food is made—and how to make it yourself—is a fun twist on the local dining scene. The courses I've attended have been some of my favorite birthday and holiday presents I've received from my husband. Though, he ultimately wins out by getting to enjoy the home-cooked meals (assuming I actually retain what I learn in class).

Where: Cambridge School of Culinary Arts, 2020 Massachusetts Ave., 617/354-2020, www.cambridgeculinary.com • Christopher Kimball's Milk Street Cooking School, 177 Milk St., 857/990-3625, www.177milkstreet.com • Stir, 103 Waltham St., 617/423-7847, www.stirboston.com

Timing: Cooking classes are highly seasonal, especially courses that rely on fresh, in-season produce. Long story short: There's not a bad time of year to book one of these classes. Demonstration sessions at Stir are so popular that it's best to plan a visit simply around the first available session.

We all know that feeling when we go to our favorite restaurant and the server sets a culinary masterpiece in front of us. Our eyes drink in the chef's artful creation, we smell the tantalizing scent of the perfectly seasoned dish, and that first bite—seared steak, Atlantic hake, vegan stew, you name it—is pure bliss. But the aspiring Ina Gartens and Bobby Flays of the world know that eating a prepared meal is only half the fun. Learning how to make tasty dishes at home can make you feel like a professional chef. Here in Boston (and a little outside), some of the city's top chefs offer a chance to do just that.

The closest experience to attending culinary school is found at the **Cambridge School of Culinary Arts,** about 20 minutes on the Red Line from Downtown Crossing. Pros teach a variety of classes depending on interest level. Some are geared toward folks simply looking for a fun night on the town learning to make things like homemade pita or Bulgarian buckwheat burgers in a $136 couples class, while others are more advanced, including $495 six-week courses on elements of cooking or $350 four-week baking courses. For those seeking to add "chef" to their resume, the CSCA offers a 37-week professional program, where tuition will set

▲ a lobster dish

▲ cinnamon buns

▲ pro night class at the Cambridge School of Culinary Arts

you back nearly $30,000. No matter which class you sign up for, you're sure to learn a lot. Wear sturdy, close-toed shoes and clothes you don't mind getting bits of food on.

Across the river, Christopher Kimball, of America's Test Kitchen and Cooks Illustrated fame, has the eponymous **Christopher Kimball's Milk Street Cooking School** headquarters in downtown Boston. Milk Street offers cooking classes, typically under $100, geared more toward the novice home cook looking to master a specific dish while learning cooking techniques such as knife and spice skills. The goal is to help cooks understand why recipes work, rather than just how to follow them. The Milk Street kitchens are also a fun introduction to the brand's impressive line of cookbooks, magazines, and pantry must-have gadgets.

For those who prefer to learn by kicking back with a glass of wine and watching a master work, Chef Barbara Lynch, arguably the biggest name in Boston dining, offers her demonstration kitchen **Stir,** located in the South End. On the same street as her B&G Oysters and Butcher Shop restaurants, Stir is an intimate way to learn the intricacies of a variety of fine-dining cuisines. The Stir space, which only seats 10 around a cooktop, quickly fills up as soon as class-

Christopher Kimball's Milk Street Cooking School

Chef Lynch

Chef Barbara Lynch is one of Boston's biggest success stories. A South Boston native, Lynch went from a troubled childhood in project housing to becoming the linchpin (pun not intended) of a dining empire responsible for some of Boston's finest kitchens. As detailed in her 2017 memoir *Out of Line: A Life of Playing with Fire*, it was not always an easy road to rise to the top and start her company, the Barbara Lynch Collective. (She even notoriously stole a city bus at the age of 13.)

But she has made a name for herself at venues like No. 9 Park—the peak of Boston fine dining—and Sportello, one of the first marquee restaurants in the city's Seaport neighborhood. Stir is one of the many ways she gives back to the city in hopes of inspiring more people to enter the cooking profession.

es are announced (check the website regularly for availability). The Stir team keeps the wine flowing, and instructors deconstruct the process of making a delectable masterpiece right before your eyes.

While Lynch's restaurants err on the side of fancy, Stir is a more relaxed, albeit business casual dress code, night out. Even though you aren't actually cooking the meal here (unless it's a specified hands-on class), chefs gladly take questions and encourage you to jot down notes so you can replicate the meal at home. The food is always delicious, but my other favorite part is perusing the cookbook shelves after the meal to find gifts to buy for friends and family.

Now, get cooking—and *bon appétit*!

Connect With...

36 Go beyond Harvard Yard in Cambridge and Somerville

12 Escape to the Boston Harbor Islands

On the Water • Fun for Families and Kids

Why Go: The Boston Harbor Islands National Recreation Area is a collection of islands in Boston Harbor. They provide a convenient, fun way to get on the water and experience local beaches without the hassle of Cape Cod traffic. Skyline views and sunset clambakes add to the fun.

Where: The Boston Harbor Islands are spread across Boston Harbor directly east of downtown Boston. Boston Harbor City Cruises offers daily service in peak summer months and seasonal weekend service through the fall from Long Wharf in downtown Boston. www.bostonharborislands.org • www.bostonharborcruises.com

Timing: Summer months are the best time to go, as ferries offer the most frequent transport to the visitable islands. Clambakes and camping are also available at this time. If you only wish to visit Spectacle Island, it's still open in the fall.

The Boston Harbor Islands National Recreation Area, a group of 34 islands and peninsulas within the city's harbor, offers island getaways without losing sight of the Boston skyline.

cruise ship in Boston Harbor

Only a small number of the islands are actually able to host visitors—Boston Harbor City Cruises provides ferry service from Long Wharf in downtown Boston to the more popular destinations like Spectacle, Thompson, Peddocks, Georges, Lovells, and Little Brewster Islands.

Visiting the islands is a choose-your-own-adventure kind of voyage. For those looking to learn about Boston's beautiful **lighthouses** (including **Boston Light,** the oldest continuously operated lighthouse in the country), the park staff and volunteer United States Coast Guard personnel provide 2-hour cruises ($35 adults; $30 students, seniors, and military; $25 kids; free for ages 3 and under) that take visitors by three lighthouses, including Boston Light, with interesting narration and history along the way.

Anyone interested in **camping** out on the islands can reserve a campsite on Bumpkin, Grape, Lovells, or Peddocks Islands. With the exception of Peddocks Island (which has yurts

▲ Boston Light

▲ sunset sail

with electricity and running water), the islands' tents-only sites offer a chance to really unplug. All campsites (and yurts), require campers to carry their own gear to and from the ferry docks.

Thompson Island is home to the **Thompson Island Events and Conference Center,** where many Boston businesses host company outings. A nice benefit of hosting events on the islands is that a portion of the fees for each event goes back to the park.

The entire Boston Harbor Islands area offers **family-friendly fun.** Kids can become junior rangers by picking up a junior ranger booklet and completing the activities to earn a badge. Tidepools and abandoned forts provide hours of entertainment. Georges Island's Fort Warren, with its hidden staircases and dark tunnels, is especially popular with kids.

Spectacle Island is my favorite. The 114-acre island has a little bit of everything for visitors to make an entire day of a trip. The views of the skyline, as well as planes landing and taking off from Logan International Airport, are incredible. A lifeguarded (in the summer), rocky beach puts parents bringing kids to the shores at ease. Rolling hills and trails provide plenty of options for runners and hikers. But one of the island's more popular activities is a **sunset clambake,** offered in partnership with Boston Harbor City Cruises, every Thursday from late-June to Labor Day. This classic New England experience can be a little pricey ($99 adults and seniors, $75 children ages 3-11, children under 3 free; reservations required), but indulging in the fresh seafood steamed over seaweed (accompanied by chowder, corn, and dessert) is the best way to enjoy your island getaway.

Boston Harbor City Cruises typically offers three daily cruises to each of the islands, departing in the morning, midday, and early afternoon from Boston's Long Wharf and returning from the islands in early, mid-, and late afternoon. An adult round-trip fare is $25, seniors ride for $23, and children under 12 for $18. Five-ride passes cost $100, and ten-ride passes go for $180. Depending on which island you go to, they can range from 20-minute rides to Spectacle Island to a 40-minute voyage to Georges Island.

Depending on the time of year, it can be chilly with the sea breeze, so be sure to bring a light jacket. For day trips, it's always smart to bring sunscreen, bug spray, snacks, drinks, and a trash bag—the islands have a carry in/carry out policy, so be a good guest and pick up after yourself!

Boston Harbor Islands in History

The Boston Harbor Islands have their place in American and cinematic history. Boston Light, erected in 1715 on Little Brewster Island, was destroyed by the British as they left Boston following their defeat in the Revolutionary War. The lighthouse was rebuilt in 1783 and remains the oldest continuously operated lighthouse in the United States.

Fort Warren, on Georges Island, served as a military training facility and war prison during the Civil War, and the complex is believed to be haunted by the "Lady in Black," the widow of a Confederate soldier.

The film *Shutter Island*, directed by Martin Scorsese and starring Leonardo DiCaprio, was filmed on Peddocks Island. The movie, based on a novel by Boston author Dennis Lehane, takes place at a Boston Harbor Island hospital for prisoners suffering from mental health disorders, though no such hospital actually exists.

Connect With...

14 Meander the Rose Kennedy Greenway

33 Play at Martin's Park

13 Rock out at the Boston Calling Music Festival

Beantown Essential • Boston Parties • Art and Culture

Why Go: By the time Memorial Day arrives, Boston has (hopefully) thawed from winter snow, which means it's time to let your hair down at a crowded music festival featuring some of your favorite bands.

Where: The Boston Calling Music Festival is held at the Harvard Athletic Complex in Allston. MBTA Red Line subway provides easy access. Get off at Harvard Station and walk south on John F. Kennedy Street • 65 N Harvard St., 617/495-3454, www.boston-calling.com

Timing: Boston Calling is a three-day festival held each Memorial Day weekend. Passes go on sale in January and sell out quickly, with single-day tickets available closer to the event—plan accordingly.

It's spring. Maybe you'd like to be at the Coachella music festival in California, but who has the time or money to make the annual trek to the Palm Springs area? (Let alone worry about

▲ live music

whether you can score tickets to the weekend with the best list of musical acts). Boston can give you all the same music festival fun without the travel expenses and hot desert sand. Mark your calendar for Memorial Day weekend and get ready to rock out at Boston Calling.

Held across five outdoor stages and an indoor arena (used as a hockey rink most months of the year) in the Harvard Athletic Complex in Allston, the three-day Boston Calling Music Festival has quickly turned into one of Boston's most-celebrated annual events since its founding in 2013.

Boston Calling hasn't hosted acts like Beyoncé (yet). But the music festival has a great variety of top or rising acts in rap, alternative, pop, and electronic music. Names like Sia, Kendrick Lamar, and Eminem have taken to the Boston Calling stages since the festival began. The crowd skews younger, but the mix of major rock and pop acts along with local bands like Dinosaur Jr. and the Sheila Divine draws people of all ages.

The festival has unique features like a Ferris wheel and beanbag chair lounges, as well as a comedy stage. Food vendors are largely talented local businesses, and Copenhagen brewery Mikkeller Beer (a favorite among local beer geeks) has a variety of beers on tap alongside local brands like Boston Beer Co., the parent company of Sam Adams. You can purchase Platinum tickets to access a special lounge and viewing area, with fancier bars and foodie delights, such as a raw oyster bar from Island Creek Oysters or Shojo's dim sum. A VIP and Platinum beer and cocktail program is also a major draw.

Keep in mind: This is a music festival, so there's a pretty good chance you'll get beer spilled on you, and, yes, that's marijuana you smell wafting all around you. (Hey, it's legal in Massachusetts!) Daytime performances can be almost tranquil, with people lounging on the lawn soaking in rays (fingers crossed for sun) and music. At nighttime, when headliners perform, things typically get rowdy with mosh pits and jam-packed crowds trying to get better views of the stage.

Lines for the bathroom, food, and alcohol are notoriously long. If the idea of standing in line for something to eat or drink really doesn't appeal to you, take advantage of the event's proximity to public transit, and enjoy a meal and a few cocktails before you head to the festival—or bring your own factory-sealed bottled water and snacks.

Passes range from around $400 for three-day general admission to just under $1,000 for VIP access during the entire weekend. Platinum passes cost $2,000. Passes usually go on sale in January ahead of the Memorial Day Weekend event, and it's best to move fast—they sell out quickly. More affordable single-day passes, around $150 for general admission, go on sale closer to the festival weekend.

Connect With...

20 Kayak the Charles River

36 Go beyond Harvard Yard in Cambridge and Somerville

14 Meander the Rose Kennedy Greenway

Get Outside • Fun for Families and Kids • Neighborhoods and City Streets

Why Go: When you need a break from the hustle and bustle of the city but can't go too far, the Rose Kennedy Greenway is a verdant respite in the heart of downtown Boston, with connections to many of the city's most diverse neighborhoods.

Where: The Greenway winds north to south from Chinatown, to the east of the Financial District, and between Government Center and the North End. • 617/292-0020, www.rosekennedygreenway.org

Timing: The Greenway is accessible year-round, but warmer months from spring through fall tend to be when most features like the Trillium Beer Garden and City Winery are in operation. Dewey Square food trucks are open during lunch hours all months of the year.

Having lived here for over a decade, I know Bostonians love to gripe about going beyond the comforts of their own neighborhoods, but the 17-acre, 1.5-mile Kennedy Greenway is worth venturing out for a true taste of Boston. This line of parks runs from Chinatown to the edge of TD Garden, with art, fountains, beer and wine gardens, and sustainable landscaping along the way.

▲ Chinatown's Paifang Gate

Start your stroll in the morning with a coffee and sweet treat from one of the bakeries in **Chinatown** along Beach Street before walking beneath the Paifang gate, passing the orange and green PlayCubes play structure as you make your way into **Uncle Frank and Auntie Kay Chin Park,** the start of the Greenway. Head north to **Dewey Square,** a lively little square with a distinctive mural wall, which changes every few months to feature a new artist. The square has food trucks, park chairs, and a pop-up wine garden called **City Winery** (summer only), which serves locally crafted wine, small bites, and beer, too, courtesy of Boston's Harpoon Brewery.

From Dewey Square, continue along the Greenway to the lush **Fort Point Channel Parks,** where you can admire many plants and trees native to New England. From there, a

fountains along the greenway

Rose Kennedy Greenway

Trillium Beer Garden

▲ the Greenway Carousel

highly popular (and seasonal) after-work and weekend hangout spot it just ahead. **Trillium Beer Garden on the Greenway,** Boston's first open-air beer garden, is a great option for those looking to enjoy a cold beer in a cool outdoor space. It also has a prime view of Boston Harbor through the expansive archway across the street at the Boston Harbor Hotel.

You won't want to miss the **Greenway Carousel,** featuring the chance to ride hand-carved wildlife (think skunks, lobsters, turtles, and owls, among other animals), in the **Wharf District Parks** farther north from Trillium. Keep an eye out for the fun Harbor Fog misting fountain by Ross Miller and the interactive *Color Commons* art installation on the way.

The final half-mile stretch of the Greenway has several important stops. The beautiful **Armenian Heritage Park,** dedicated to victims of Armenian Genocide, celebrates the immigrant experience in Boston. Farther north is the **Zippora Potter Atkins Marker,** which marks the spot where the only 17th-century woman of African descent purchased land in Boston. There are also sweeping sculptures and fountains bridging the historically Italian North End and the more business-oriented Faneuil Hall and Government Center neighborhoods.

The Big Dig

The Central Artery/Tunnel Project, better known as the Big Dig, was a mammoth highway project built over the course of the 1990s and early 2000s that tunneled Interstate 93 under downtown Boston and replaced its formerly elevated highway stretch with the linear Rose Kennedy Greenway. Exit cars, enter a much-improved Boston street-level experience for pedestrians.

The Big Dig was expensive. Like...a $22(ish) billion price tag and 190% over budget expensive. But was it worth it? It's hard to find many people who would say it wasn't. The multibillion-dollar project was supposed to alleviate traffic—it hasn't—but the park is unquestionably a resounding success. Its creation also unlocked the potential for another popular Boston neighborhood, the Seaport. Money pit or not, the Greenway is a big reason why Boston has boomed in recent years.

This is a great spot to relax with a book and a meal from the nearby **Boston Public Market,** or to kill time before a date at one of the North End's nearby Italian eateries.

Restrooms are available at various points along the Greenway. There are also plenty of public transit stops nearby and a water taxi service at Rowes Wharf and the North Station/TD Garden end of the Greenway. Traffic in the area can be a pain, so take advantage of these options.

Connect With...

6 Feast in Chinatown
24 Customize the Freedom Trail
33 Play at Martin's Park

15 See Broadway hits-to-be
in the Theater District

Art and Culture

Why Go: Boston's theaters can give audiences a first look at the next big thing to hit Broadway as well as more established productions just as they begin to hit the road on a national tour—often for lower ticket prices than what you'd find in New York City.

Where: The American Repertory Theater, 64 Brattle St., Cambridge, 617/547-8300, www.americanrepertorytheater.org • Emerson Culter Majestic Theatre, 219 Tremont St., Boston, 617/824-8400, www.emersontheatres.org • Emerson Colonial Theatre, 106 Boylston St., Boston, 888/616-0272, www.emersoncolonialtheatre.com • Boch Center – Wang Theatre, 270 Tremont St., Boston, 617/482-9393, www.bochcenter.org

Timing: The Boston theater scene offers year-round entertainment.

Boston's Theater District may not be quite the neon-lit spectacle that is Times Square, but this concentration of venues small and large still packs a theatrical punch. Marquees blare nightly with signs of the performance du jour, and trendy eateries and bars buzz with theatergoers before or after the big act. Performances on any given night in local theaters range from a mix of touring Broadway shows like Hamilton or Chicago, to smaller, locally developed acts. More recently, Broadway producers have returned to the historic practice of workshopping musicals in Boston before moving the fine-tuned finished products down to the Great White Way.

Greater Boston boasts a variety of major theaters, from the **American Repertory Theater (A.R.T.)** in Harvard Square to a greater concentration of venues, including the **Cutler Majestic Theatre** and **Colonial Theatre** downtown. **The Wang Theatre,** which seats 3,500, is the city's largest—and its opulent Versailles-inspired lobby is almost just as entertaining as whatever takes place on the main stage. Architecture buffs will enjoy the Beaux-Arts feel of the Cutler Majestic, while the Colonial, which opened in 1900, is Boston's oldest continuously running theater. It hosts a mix of touring performers and Broadway shows as well as student productions from Emerson College, which owns the theater.

Given its proximity to New York City, Boston has traditionally played an important role in

Waitress at the American Repertory Theater

Jagged Little Pill at the American Repertory Theater

developing Broadway productions. Producers would workshop and test out a musical or play here and iron out any issues before moving four hours down the highway to Broadway. Richard Rodgers, of the famed Rodgers & Hammerstein composer duo, used to say he wouldn't even try to open a can of tomatoes without testing it in Boston first.

The 2011 production of *The Gershwins' Porgy and Bess*, starring Audra McDonald, tested at the A.R.T. before heading to Broadway—76 years after a similar pre-New York test happened at the Colonial Theater in Boston. The A.R.T. also tested other highly popular musicals like *Waitress* and the Alanis Morissette-inspired *Jagged Little Pill*. Other pre-Broadway debuts in recent years have included Moulin Rouge, musician David Byrne's *American Utopia*, and the Sarah Jessica Parker and Matthew Broderick-starring *Plaza Suite*.

Over the years, Boston lost some of its pre-Broadway testing to other cities like Chicago and Washington, D.C., but redevelopment and new ownership behind several local theaters like the Colonial have helped to revive the trend. The Broadway testing is a point of local pride, and

▲ Cutler Majestic Theatre

Banned in Boston

Thanks to Boston's Puritanical roots, the theater scene was a late bloomer; plays weren't even legal in the city until the late 1700s. This led to some under-the-table theatrical operations, disguised with such names as Exhibition Hall or the Boston Museum, according to records from the Boston Athenaeum. "Banned in Boston" was even a badge of pride from Boston theater lovers. Luckily, the love of the stage eventually conquered over censorship.

Massachusetts leaders have even considered adding a theater tax credit to its already popular film tax credit to lure more stage shows to the area.

If you want to be part of a pre-Broadway test audience, keep tabs on www.boston-theater.com for information about which productions are available throughout the year. Ticket prices to Boston productions of these shows are significantly less than on Broadway: you could get a $25 ticket to *Jagged Little Pill* when it debuted at the A.R.T. compared to prices well over $100 on Broadway. But as with any production, tickets to the more popular shows are hard to come by at first. However, the nonprofit ArtsBoston BosTix (560 Boylston St., https://artsboston.org/sellbostix/) sells same-day and discounted tickets at booths in Faneuil Hall downtown and Copley Square in Back Bay. All proceeds are reinvested into the Boston arts community.

Connect With...

6 Feast in Chinatown
22 Splurge on Newbury Street

16 Dine at a Boston food hall

Drink and Dine

Why Go: For those of us who can never seem to make up our minds on what to eat, having multiple restaurants under a single roof can be a life (and cravings) saver.

Where: Boston Public Market, 100 Hanover St., 617/973-4909, www.bostonpublicmarket.org • Time Out Boston, 401 Park Dr., 978/393-8088, www.timeout.com • Eataly, 800 Bolyston St., 617/807-7300, www.eataly.com

Timing: I personally love visiting food halls when it's too cold outside for patio dining, as many of the vendors in local food halls happen to have the best outdoor seating at their "regular" restaurants. But places like Time Out Market Boston also have outdoor beer halls, which are best visited in the summer.

It wasn't long ago when local critics bemoaned that Boston wasn't as fun with its food and bar scene as bigger cities like New York or Los Angeles. Boston lacked their variety in the kitch-

▲ Terra at Eataly

en and the innovative opportunities to taste-test delectable creations from some of the best chefs in the business. Not wanting to be outdone, Boston got in on the food hall game. Today, diners can sample various cuisines and pick up artisanal goods in mini-restaurants, food stalls, and shops all under the same roof in several parts of the city.

The **Boston Public Market** near Government Center opened in 2015 and was the city's original modern food hall, attracting popular local names in dining like **Bon Me,** which serves Vietnamese-style sandwiches, and **Union Square Donuts,** a creative donut shop, along-

side lesser-known tasty spots like **Mo'Rockin Fusion,** which serves up innovative Moroccan dishes, and **Inna's Kitchen,** a family-owned Jewish deli. There are typically 30 vendors at the market at any given time, and all of them come from New England and source their products from the region—truly local delicacies! The market is housed in a modern downtown building, so aisles are spacious and able to handle bustling crowds passing through along the Freedom

▲ pizza at Eataly

▲ Boston Public Market

▲ Time Out Market Boston

Trail or from nearby offices. Even if you aren't hungry, it's worth a visit to buy gifts like local honey or bowls and cutting boards made from discarded local trees—however, do try to save enough room for at least one Union Square donut. Expect to see more tourists at the Boston Public Market than other local food halls due to its location directly on the Freedom Trail.

Time Out Market Boston launched as part of a major redevelopment in the Fenway neighborhood's western side in recent years. The food hall is a modern industrial space occupying an airy corner of what was once a Sears distribution facility built in 1929. The market features 15 booths from major local chefs like Michael Schlow and Tim Cushman. From deli sandwiches to gelato to Mediterranean fare, the Time Out Market offers a wide variety of dining options, which is a major step forward for foodies in a neighborhood that not too long ago was best known for Fenway Frank hot dogs served at the ballpark. Given its tucked-away location past Fenway Park, far away from other touristy attractions like the Freedom Trail, Time Out Market is a local-focused market most residents actually visit. You'll usually find me volleying between the Mediterranean bowls from **Anoush'ella** and the meatballs from **Michael Schlow's Italian Kitchen.**

The all-Italian emporium **Eataly** arrived in Back Bay at the Prudential Center shopping mall a year after Boston Public Market officially opened, and it quickly amassed a following of aficionados of Italian cuisine. A high-end restaurant, gelato shops, cafés, a butcher, a fishmonger, a cheesemonger (which can get surprisingly pricy for a nice block of parmesan), and a wine shop are just a few of the offerings at this bright, luxurious market. Yes, even the pasta shelves and produce stands at Eataly look like something out of a magazine. Take advantage of the food hall/Italian specialty market's focus on one cuisine and find novelty items (red pepper-infused spaghetti, anyone? I'll take four packs, please!) not typically found on the shelves of your local supermarket. Some of my favorite times with friends and family visiting from out of town have involved sharing bread, cheese, and meats over a bottle of rosé at one of the counters in the central market. However, it's always fun to go the extra mile and spend a little bit more at **Terra,** the market's third-floor restaurant packed with hanging plants and expansive skylights—you'll almost feel like you're dining al fresco as you enjoy that bite of juicy lamb or pillowy beet gnocchi.

Time Out Market has the most seating of any of the markets, especially when you factor

Food Halls to the Rescue

Boston's dining scene is at a bit of a crossroads, as rents have been exploding and customer tastes are changing. This shuttered many of the city's most historic restaurants, like the No Name Restaurant and Durgin-Park. Even L'Espalier, often seen as a recession-proof kitchen due to its appeal to high-end traffic, closed at the end of 2018.

The high cost associated with opening and maintaining a restaurant in Boston drove many chefs away to places like Portland, Maine, and Providence, Rhode Island. But city and state leaders, both in the public and private sector, seem to recognize the cost problem and ensuing chef drain to smaller, more affordable municipalities. Food trucks took off in recent years, and developers have courted many of these eateries into brick-and-mortar spaces (Bon Me is one of these success stories).

Food halls are seen as a similar incubator space, with Time Out Market being a leader. Hopefully, it isn't too late to save mom-and-pop operators and foster the next generation of rising kitchen talent.

in the 6,000-square-foot patio outside. It can be a little bit of a race to find elbow room in more condensed settings like Eataly and the Boston Public Market, but these locations are conveniently located near parks or plazas if you want to sit outside on a nice day. Given the high volume of visitors at each of the markets, credit cards are best to speed things along when it comes time to pay. Each of the markets has ample restrooms.

Keep an eye on the Boston food hall scene—it's only getting bigger and better!

Connect With...

14 Meander the Rose Kennedy Greenway

26 Explore Fenway beyond the Red Sox

32 Get to know the Boston Brahmin in Back Bay and Beacon Hill

17 Gallery hop in SoWa

Art and Culture • Neighborhoods and City Streets

Why Go: SoWa offers a range of options, from brunch to shopping. But take time for a visit focused exclusively on this district's dense concentration of artist's galleries and studios.

Where: SoWa technically means South of Washington, but the arts district is largely along Harrison Avenue between Malden and Berkeley Streets. There is no direct public transportation access, but the MBTA Silver Line runs nearby along Washington Street.
• www.sowaboston.com

Timing: Anytime between May and late October are peak SoWa months, especially on weekends. But shops are largely open year-round, and seasonal events around winter holidays do pop up.

Like all great arts districts, the area south of Washington, or SoWa, blossomed as a haven for creativity due to its converted lofts and once-affordable rent. Newbury Street in Back Bay was, and continues to be, another gallery-centric part of the city, but many of the contemporary art galleries migrated toward the South End. SoWa was originally home to a mix of utility plants and warehouses for manufacturing goods like pianos and other industrial uses. But after years of neglect, artists poured in and reimagined these spaces into studios, galleries, and boutique shops. Today, the neighborhood leaders work diligently to protect the area's artsy identity.

The SoWa Art and Design District is home to more than 200 working artists across all mediums. The non-profit SoWa Artists Guild is an association of nearly 60 studio artists, who work within the neighborhood and showcase their work with events like SoWa First Fridays, the SoWa Art Walk, and SoWa Open Studios. Most of the galleries feature contemporary art, from sculpture to painting and photography.

The **First Fridays** events happen, as you might guess, the first Friday of each month from 5pm to 9pm and are a fun way to meet artists and consider splurging on a new masterpiece. These aren't stuffy gallery experiences so much as they're a Friday night block party, with live music performed along many of the open ground-floor galleries at the SoWa Artists

International Poster Gallery

First Friday at Abigail Ogilvy Gallery

Thayer Street

▲ Thayer Street

Guild buildings at 450 and 460 Harrison Ave. Artists are present, so it's a good chance to meet the creative force behind the masterpiece and chat over a glass of wine or a passed appetizer. The events are often a reflection of the surrounding South End neighborhood, which means a diverse crowd of all ages. Consider making reservations at nearby restaurants like Burro Bar (1357 Washington St., 617/426-9300, www.burrobarboston.com) or Bar Mezzana (360 Harrison Ave., 617/530-1770, www.barmezzana.com) for when you're hungry after admiring the local artwork.

SoWa Art Walk is an annual event that usually takes up an entire spring weekend in May and showcases local working artists as well as talent from around the world. Similar to the First Friday events, SoWa Art Walk features open galleries and opportunities to meet the artists, but this is a much bigger event that includes more galleries beyond the SoWa Artists Guild building. Stroll the event to enjoy art as well as food and handicrafts. (I typed this on top of a refurbished desk I bought at the market several years ago.) Admission is free, but bring your wallet to purchase art, snacks, and gifts.

The **SoWa Open Market,** a Sunday farmers and artists market runs from May through October. The venue is a great place to find handmade gifts, shop for organic ingredients for dinner, or even just grab a meal with friends in the expanded food truck and beer garden in the Central Power Station building off Harrison Avenue. Crowds get bigger with each year, but so does the entertainment: musical acts are also sometimes part of the Sunday SoWa mix.

Don't feel like you can only visit galleries during special events. Any day is a good day to wander the neighborhood in search of artistic eye candy. SoWa galleries, generally found on Harrison Street between West Dedham and Berkeley Streets, are open every day of the week. Thayer Street, a side street off Harrison, also has a heavy mix of galleries and boutique shops and serves as the turn-off point to get to the SoWa Open Market.

As the area has become more of a residential hub, furniture stores, architecture studios, and high-end salons have opened. But unlike other parts of the city, SoWa strives to maintain its hip image by avoiding chain stores or restaurants from appearing in any of these former warehouses.

Connect With...

㉙ Brunch around the World in the South End

18 Cheer on runners at the Boston Marathon

Beantown Essential • Boston Parties • Get Outside

Why Go: Sure, there are other marathons and regattas in cities around the world, but there's only one Boston Marathon and only one Head of the Charles. Both competitions are something athletes in their respective sports strive to qualify for, and the spectatorship for both is unparalleled.

Where: The Boston Marathon starts in the western suburb of Hopkinton and ends in Copley Square in Boston's Back Bay neighborhood, www.baa.org • The Head of the Charles starts in the Charles River Basin (boats line up under the Massachusetts Avenue bridge between Boston and Cambridge) and runs past the shores of Harvard University's campus, www.hocr.org

Timing: The Boston Marathon is usually held the third Monday of April each year and the Head of the Charles is typically held the penultimate weekend of each October.

Boston is known as "Titletown," thanks to the prowess of its pro sports teams like the Celtics, Red Sox, Bruins, and the Patriots. But professional athletes aren't the only ones working up a sweat in this city. The Boston Marathon and Head of the Charles Regatta draw the entire city (and visitors from around the world) in droves to the streets of Greater Boston and shores of the Charles River.

▲ the Charles River

The Boston Marathon, held the third Monday of April each year, runs 26.2 miles from the western suburb of Hopkinton all the way to Copley Square in the heart of Boston's Back Bay neighborhood. Runners range from elite qualifiers who complete the course in just over two hours to those who need closer to eight. Participants say Boston is among the toughest marathon courses around, due to its late-stage Heartbreak Hill, a nearly half-mile ascent shortly after mile 20—but some say that makes it even more rewarding.

Marathon Monday is a cherished regional holiday (otherwise known as Patriots' Day), and residents and visitors pack the sidelines to cheer on friends, family, and even strangers who are

Boston Marathon

runners along the route

Boston Marathon enthusiasm

making their way to the finish line. From the Wellesley College Scream Tunnel (where kisses are offered, too) to the throng of Boston College students cheering those who make it to their front gate at the top of Heartbreak Hill, there is plenty of encouragement along the way. For spectators who plan ahead, some of the best spots to watch and cheer on runners include bars and restaurants in Kenmore Square and along the final stretch of Boylston Street before the finish line.

For race participants, the marathon itself is only part of the fun. Thanks to the Boston Athletic Association, runners can also enjoy a race expo with over 200 vendors, a pre-race dinner, and a post-race party (presented by Samuel Adams).

If you want to get involved but you're not interested in running 26.2 miles, you can sign up to volunteer, helping with registration or handing out much-needed cups of water along the route.

In October, Boston plays host to another unique sporting event: **The Head of the**

▲ the Head of the Charles

Charles, one of the world's largest regattas. The event draws rowers from all over who sprint from the Charles River Basin along a windy, 3-mile course upriver.

Singles, doubles, four-person, and eight-person boats all jockey for victory in this two-day championship, which is among the more preppy of New England events. Brands like Brooks Brothers sponsor tents along the side of the course, offering spectators a chance to sip champagne while athletes row by.

Less posh ways to view the race are just as (if not more) fun. Pack a picnic and find a spot along one of the bridges over the river to cheer for rowers going by at impressive speeds. The Boston University Bridge between Cambridge and Brighton is close to the start of the race and the John W. Weeks Bridge between Cambridge and Allston is a pivotal point where boats have to steer a corner (and often crash).

Of the two sporting events, the Boston Marathon, the world's oldest annual marathon, certainly reigns supreme. The event was reportedly inspired by the revival of the marathon as a sporting event at the 1896 Summer Olympics in Athens, and the Boston Marathon was born a year later.

Connect With...

6 Feast in Chinatown
30 Stroll on the Esplanade

19 Geek out at the Museum of Science

Fun for Families and Kids • Art and Culture

Why Go: Don't let the name fool you: during the day, the Museum of Science attracts a mix of schoolchildren and science fanatics to its 700 exhibits, but even club kids can find something here, with the museum's nighttime events like light shows on the Charles Hayden Planetarium dome set to a soundtrack of current hits.

Where: The Museum of Science (1 Science Park, 617/723-2500, www.mos.org) is located in Boston on the Charles River Dam Bridge between Boston's West End and Lechmere Square in Cambridge. Science Park station on the MBTA's Green Line is a four-minute walk southeast of the museum.

Timing: It's always a good time to visit the museum; however, if you're looking to avoid crowds, steer clear of summer months and holidays.

There's a lot about the Museum of Science that screams school field trip—which is precisely why it's worth visiting. The rather nondescript red-brick building on the Charles River Dam along the river basin's northeastern edge is packed with hundreds of exhibits, the Charles Hayden Planetarium, an IMAX theater, and the Live Animal Care Center (the museum is also an accredited zoo with 120 animals).

It can be tough for a first-time visitor to figure out where to begin amid all 700 of the museum's exhibits; I suggest starting with a little bit of local flare. The **"Wicked Smart: Invented in the Hub"** exhibit in the museum's first hall (the Blue Wing) just off the main lobby features the creations of Boston-area inventors and was inspired by the fact Massachusetts is considered one of the most innovative states by magazines like Bloomberg. Some of the exhibit's featured items include RoboBees, created at Harvard to pollinate flowers, and a robot cheetah capable of running and jumping over obstacles, developed by a team at MIT.

Further into the Blue Wing from the Wicked Smart exhibit is the **Theater of Electricity,** where museum staffers conjure up images of Greek gods with the help of a Van de Graaff Generator, a machine that collects, separates, and moves negative charges between

▲ Museum of Science

▲ Yawkey Gallery

▲ Hall of Human Life

two aluminum spheres, creating indoor lightning in the process. Don't fret: it's entirely safe, though it can get a little loud.

The animal center on the museum's lower level offers a mix of viewings through windows and interactive experiences via the museum's live presentation programming. The 20-minute **Science Live presentations** include up-close encounters with some of the venue's reptiles, amphibians, and other animals.

The Museum of Science also takes part in a species **conservation program,** breeding cotton-top tamarins as part of an initiative to preserve the population and their native habitat in Colombia. There is also a conservation program for the more regionally native northern red-bellied cooter—a type of turtle found in Plymouth County, south of the city. The museum helps raise the baby turtles for their first year until they are better equipped to stave off predators like skunks or raccoons.

Other museum highlights include an engineering workshop, the biology-focused Hall of

a cotton-top tamarin

Origins: The Museum of Science

The Museum of Science was originally named the Boston Society of Natural History and was once housed in an ornate building in Boston's Back Bay that is now a Restoration Hardware furniture store. The Museum of Science got its present-day name and location in 1951.

While the museum has been renovated several times over the years, it got its biggest financial boost in 2016 when former New York City Mayor Michael Bloomberg donated $50 million, the largest financial gift in museum history.

Human Life, an indoor park with playground equipment, and a nanotechnology exhibit with interactive stations.

Grown-ups, don't feel like you have to limit your activities to the child-friendly museum exhibits. The Museum of Science lets its hair down after dark in the Charles Hayden Planetarium. The venue's daytime shows can take visitors to Mars or show breathtaking imagery of various moons in our solar system. But at night, the planetarium offers **Music Under the Dome,** a light show geared toward adults and set to the music of artists like Beyoncé and Prince. The 40-minute show is a great pregame before you head off for a night at bars in nearby East Cambridge or Boston's West or North Ends.

If you have enough time to spare after your day at the museum, you can hop aboard a **Boston Duck Tour** (www.bostonducktours.com) directly outside next to the Tyrannosaurus rex statue in front of the Charles Hayden Planetarium. These 80-minute tours aboard an amphibious vehicle take you throughout the city and even into the Charles River. The tours are highly popular with people of all ages, but especially with children, who even get a chance to steer the "boat" when it's in the river. The Duck Boat will drop you back off in front of the museum when you finish.

Connect With...

4 Walk the Black Heritage Trail
25 Eat Italian food on Hanover Street
30 Stroll on the Esplanade

20 Kayak the Charles River

Get Outside • On the Water

Why Go: The Charles River offers some of the most photographable views of Boston's famous Back Bay, Beacon Hill, and Cambridge neighborhoods.

Where: The Charles runs from the western suburb of Hopkinton (where the Boston Marathon begins) all the way to Boston Harbor. Within Boston, most kayak rentals are concentrated in the Allston/Brighton neighborhood, and Cambridge's Kendall Square.
• Paddle Boston, 15 Broad Way, 617/965-5110, www.paddleboston.com

Timing: Summer is typically the busiest time on the water, but also one of the better times to rent a kayak, as the weather is most predictably warm. The latter part of spring or early part of fall are also ideal, as there will be fewer crowds and likely temperate weather.

Today, Bostonians love the Charles River just as much as they adore Boston Harbor. But the river hasn't always been a source of such civic pride. Similar to the harbor, the Charles was once so heavily polluted that nobody would dare go near it, let alone kayak down its currents. Clean-up efforts began in the 1960s, and it was deemed perfectly safe to swim in by the early 2000s. Now, you can see college crews rowing up and down the river at sunrise, or, a much more leisurely activity, kayakers enjoying the picturesque waters.

When the city gets crowded, if it's been a stressful week, or if there just isn't enough time to get away for a weekend, I'll pop over to **Paddle Boston**'s Kendall Square launch in Cambridge to rent a kayak and get on the water.

The standard kayak rental period is three hours ($38 per-person day rate, $20 per-person evening rate), the perfect amount of time to explore the entire 9-mile Charles River Basin between Back Bay and Cambridge—and get great photos of the Boston skyline while you're at it. As you peacefully paddle along, enjoying your cardio and arm workout, admire the gold dome of the **Massachusetts State House,** Boston's tallest building (200 Clarendon Street), which locals still call the **John Hancock Tower,** and marvel at the iconic neon Citgo sign over **Fenway Park,** all visible from the water.

▲ kayakers passing Harvard University

Skilled paddlers could make it up to the **Harvard campus** shoreline and back. But be alert: tour boats and many recreational and competitive sailing boats from colleges like MIT, Harvard, and Boston University are in the water, too.

Paddle Boston offers a variety of kayaking tour options, including sunset and skyline adventures. They also have catering services to pair your paddles with meals from local restaurants. The options include tasty pizza, Southern-inspired barbeque, and even a classic New England clambake.

If you're paddling during the day, don't forget your sunscreen. Sunglasses and hats are recommended, but bring a strap so you don't lose your glasses in the water. Wear clothes you don't mind getting a little wet, including a windbreaker or light jacket. Pack water and snacks if you like (alcohol is not permitted), and take advantage of the Paddle Boston's dry bag rentals ($1) for phones and other electronics, to avoid an unfortunate post-paddle rice bag dry-out situation. If you drive to Kendall Square (350 Kendall St.), be sure to bring money for parking.

▲ kayaks for rent on the Charles River

River Clean-Up

The Charles River today is known for its picturesque waterfront parks and running trails. But to say the Charles River went through an ugly duckling phase is putting it mildly. Sewage and wastewater used to flow into the river to the point that historian Bernard DeVoto claimed the river was "unlikely to be mistaken for water." Toxic chemicals that poured into the river even turned it various colors. Music group the Standells' 1960s hit "Dirty Water" is about the Charles.

Sometime around the song's release, clean-up efforts began and, by the early 2000s, regional and state leaders said the entire river was safe for swimming. Along with kayaking, the Charles is home to one of Boston's most famous sporting weekends: the Head of the Charles Regatta, which draws thousands of rowers in late October.

Connect With...

30 Stroll on the Esplanade

32 Get to know the Boston Brahmin in Back Bay and Beacon Hill

36 Go beyond Harvard Yard in Cambridge and Somerville

21 Taste-test chowdah

Drink and Dine • Beantown Essential

Why Go: Boston's dining scene includes some of the best seafood in the entire U.S., so hopping around on an unofficial bar-and-chowder crawl is a great way to explore some of the best and most historic dining rooms in the entire region.

Where: It's probably more difficult to find a neighborhood in Boston without a venue selling chowder. I tend to break bread...er, oyster crackers...in some of the city's more established neighborhoods—the chowder just feels more authentic when you're elbow-to-elbow with the next table! Places like the South End, North End, and Seaport are my favorites for this creamy nirvana in a cup.

Timing: Oysters and clams, if handled properly, are generally always in season. However, I tend to devour more chowder in colder months like the fall and winter (even spring is crisp in New England!).

New England clam chowder is best associated with seafood shacks from Massachusetts to Maine, but the creamy take on chowder is said to have been introduced to the region by French or British settlers in the 1700s. The soup gained its star status in local dining rooms, and it even got a passing mention in Herman Melville's *Moby-Dick*.

Its popularity has continued thanks to Legal Sea Foods chowder appearing on every presidential inauguration menu since Ronald Reagan—though there was a brief moment ahead of Donald Trump's 2017 inauguration when the chowder was reportedly not going to be served. The snub was later rolled back, and the chowder lived to see another incoming president. "We're just happy that the tradition continues," Legal Sea Foods CEO Roger Berkowitz told *The Boston Globe* at the time. "It's not partisan chowder."

You've probably eaten clam chowder at some point, but if you haven't had authentic New England clam chowder, you don't know chowdah. That tomato-y slop Manhattanites try to claim is a variation of chowder or those imitation varieties with watery broth, barely cooked potatoes, and gray chunks of clam all give chowder a bad name. This is New England. Welcome to the land of heavy cream and hearty clams. You want a rich, creamy broth that almost borders

chowder

B&G Oysters

the Barking Crab

on the consistency of mashed potatoes. The clams should be fresh and swimming in the cream alongside chunks of bacon, leeks, potatoes, and as much pepper and oyster crackers as your heart desires.

When it comes to devouring this delicious dish, eat it hot. There's nothing worse in the whole clam world than a cold chowder. Don't burn yourself, of course, but don't loiter in your consumption, either. For those who consume on the faster side, the chowder stays hot, and the oyster crackers retain a crunch with each bite. It is meant to be enjoyed as an appetizer (or a stopgap snack in the late afternoon on a frigid January day), after all. Luxuriate later, on your entrée.

Now let's talk about where to find the best chowder around. While lines out the door may scream tourist trap, this is often just a sign of a good chowder spot (as is the aroma of salty waterfront air and heavy cream from the kitchen). However, I typically avoid some of the generic restaurants in the heart of Faneuil Hall, as the chowder seems more like food court cuisine than an authentic foodie experience.

The most popular chowder will forever belong to **Legal Sea Foods** (https://www.legalseafoods.com). Legal chowder's status as a mainstay on the menu of presidential inauguration balls may make it seem fancy, but it's actually the most accessible, thanks to the company's numerous restaurants throughout Boston and greater New England. Originally a Cambridge fish market, Legal Cash Market eventually expanded to include an adjoining restaurant known as Legal Sea Foods. The company has since ballooned into a chain of seafood restaurants. The chowder here is beloved and once you taste it, you'll find out why.

Next up is Chef Barbara Lynch's **B&G Oysters** (550 Tremont St., 617/423-0550, http://bandgoysters.com/) in the South End. It's a favorite haunt of mine, where I go to think about life, sip a glass of Sancerre, and devour a cup of B&G's delectable chowder—complete with spicy croutons. Summer at B&G is even better, as you can enjoy your chowder in the back garden. The open-concept restaurant, which launched in the early 2000s, was a departure from Lynch's ultra-luxury, sometimes-stuffy No. 9 Park in Beacon Hill. At B&G you can watch your steaming chowder get ladled into a porcelain bowl next to white fish searing on the grill.

Over in the North End, **Neptune Oyster** (63 Salem St., 617/742-3474, https://www.neptuneoyster.com) is where you arrive at 10am to maybe snag a seat at the bar for lunch—

Farming Clams

The fishing industry and aquaculture of New England is big business. Given the increase in regulations for fishing offshore, many fisherfolk have instead turned to shellfish farming. Clam and oyster farms are prevalent in tidal areas throughout New England, particularly in Cape Cod. Clam larvae are placed on fine-mesh screens in open-ended cylinders. Algae-rich water is pushed through the opening to allow the clams to grow. Once they reach a sufficient size, the growing clams are moved to mesh trays and placed in nursery rafts in salt water within a tidal area of the harbor. When the clams are about the size of a fingernail, they are moved to a wider, protected growing area to finish their development before being dug and bagged for consumption in your next cup of chowder. Aquatic farm-to-table dining at its finest!

which starts an hour later. But this hole-in-the-wall-turned-glam-restaurant serves up tasty chowder each day using Wellfleet oysters, and it's the perfect seafood entry point before exploring Neptune's extensive raw bar (Sidenote: Neptune may be known more for its oysters, but the lobster roll here is a great addition to any visit!). Neptune Oyster is the kind of restaurant that attracts tourists but still feels like a longstanding neighborhood hangout.

For those wanting a little more outdoor excitement with their seafood, thank the team at the **Barking Crab** (88 Sleeper St., 617/426-2722, http://barkingcrab.com). This carnival tent-covered seafood shack on the shores of Fort Point Channel has, since its opening day in 1994, witnessed glass-and-steel towers rise around it as the Seaport neighborhood has changed. But things at the Barking Crab remain decidedly raucous, filling, and fried. Locals and fans come for the fried seafood or lobster baskets, but chowder and a cold glass of Harpoon IPA (brewed on the other side of the neighborhood) is the ultimate treat.

Connect With...

5 Marvel at the Boston Public Library
14 Meander the Rose Kennedy Greenway
17 Gallery hop in SoWA

22 Splurge on Newbury Street

Neighborhoods and City Streets

Why Go: Newbury Street is Boston's high street of upscale shopping that also extends to a funkier end of shops the further you walk from the Boston Public Garden. Even those not intending to shop 'til they drop should make a point of strolling Newbury with coffee in hand simply for the people-watching, and to get a sense of Boston's best-known thoroughfare.

Where: Newbury Street's main stretch of retail runs for about a mile east to west, from Arlington Street at the Boston Public Garden in the east to Massachusetts Avenue in the west.

Timing: The best times of year to visit are in warmer months, particularly from May through September, when there is outdoor dining and occasional programming that shuts off the street to car traffic.

New York City's Fifth Avenue is known for its monstrous-sized stores and buzzing traffic. Rodeo Drive in Beverly Hills features more of a see-and-be-seen crowd. Boston's Newbury Street is no less fashionable; it just does things a little more subtly. Most of the stores lining this shopping mecca are in brownstones rather than palatial retail outlets. But don't let the subdued shop fronts and signage fool you—the prices are still sky-high in many instances. Visitors can find everything from in-season couture to used records in Boston's iconic shopping hub.

The general rule of thumb is the further east you are on Newbury Street, the more likely you are to need deep pockets to enjoy the retail. But don't be intimidated—there's still plenty of fun to be had on this retail row without breaking the bank.

Start your shopping spree at the northeast end of Newbury Street, near Boston Public Garden, and head southwest. The glitziest of names in fashion, from **Chanel** to **Burberry** to **Valentino,** are found within the **first block** of Newbury, between **Arlington Street** and **Berkeley Street.** (It makes sense that some of the city's most expensive real estate and the first Four Seasons Hotel in town are all located in this power block of shops. Somehow a day

Anthropologie

Chanel

Newbury Street

of power-shopping feels even better if you can drown out the terror of your next credit card statement with a glass of wine at the Four Seasons bar.)

Even if you aren't in the market for couture fashion, it's always fun to pop into local jeweler **Shreve, Crump & Low** (39 Newbury St., 617/267-9100, www.shrevecrumpandlow.com) on this block. While this three-story flagship isn't the original location, Shreve, Crump & Low has been the Boston gentry's go-to spot for watches, jewels, and home goods since 1796. It's window-shopping at its finest, and salespeople here aren't pushy in the least.

The enormous **Restoration Hardware flagship** (234 Berkeley St., 857/239-7202, www.rh.com), formerly the Museum of National History, at the corner of Berkeley and Newbury offers four floors of high-end houseware-gawking. The cavernous store is worth a stroll, either for perusing the restored historic building that dates to 1864 or just to relax on one of the exceptionally soft couches positioned throughout the entire gallery—it almost seems disrespectful to call this a store.

Okay, we're only two blocks in, but I'm always peckish, so this is typically when I pop into **L.A. Burdick Chocolates** (220 Clarendon St., 617/303-0113, www.burdickchocolate.com) around the corner in the 108 Newbury Street shopping mall for a coffee or hot chocolate and, of course, a few sweet treats like the handmade chocolate mice or penguins (no actual animals are harmed in the making of these sweet masterpieces).

Walk farther southwest on Newbury Street, and you'll find major brands like **Ralph Lauren, Lilly Pulitzer,** and **Anthropologie.** While these aren't necessarily the most affordable places to shop, at least your wallet will get more of a breather than it would in the couture cluster near the Public Garden. This also just so happens to be where the nearby restaurants and cafés begin to skew younger (read: a little less expensive) with clientele.

Saltie Girl (281 Dartmouth St., 617/267-0691, www.saltiegirl.com), at Dartmouth and Newbury, is one of my favorite spots for seafood as it churns out creative spins on local fish (three words: lobster and waffles) as well as tinned fish. No, this isn't StarKist tuna; rather, it's an extensive line-up of Portuguese-style presentations of fish like tuna or scallops in various marinades and served with bread and pepper jam. A block west, you'll find **Stephanie's on Newbury** (190 Newbury St., 617/236-0990, www.stephaniesonnewbury.com), arguably one of the best spots for al fresco brunch on the weekends.

Newbury Street Retail: Going Strong

As with a lot of brick-and-mortar retail, Newbury Street has struggled in recent years and lost some of its uber-popularity. Major chains bailed for suburban mall locations, and renovations at the nearby Copley Place and Prudential Center malls snapped up major designers like Versace and Saint Laurent, names one would normally expect on the tony first block of Newbury.

But Newbury's demise is over-exaggerated in the local press. Walk along the thoroughfare on a weekend afternoon and you'll see crowded restaurants and bars, bustling stores, and, sure, maybe the occasional empty storefront or two. But in the Amazon era, what high street isn't struggling just a tad?

As you continue your stroll, things take a decidedly hipper turn somewhere after Gloucester Street. Nearby colleges like Boston University and Berklee College of Music give this stretch of Newbury a more eclectic, college-age feel, and **Diesel Jeans, Urban Outfitters,** and **Uniqlo,** all popular with the 20-something crowd, have major shops here. Restaurants on this block, like **Sonsie** (327 Newbury St., 617/351-2500, www.sonsieboston.com), also cater to a more see-and-be-seen crowd, attracting patrons who want to take advantage of the expansive windows (okay, maybe things do get a little Beverly Hills in Beantown). For a quick bite, **Pavement Coffeehouse** (286 Newbury St., 617/859-9515, www.pavementcoffeehouse.com) is a good spot for a coffee or jalapeño bagel on the go.

Massachusetts Avenue marks the end of the main shopping drag—but there's so much to see along this bustling street that you can always turn around and walk back the way you came to see what you missed on the way (or to grab more treats).

Connect With...

5 Marvel at the Boston Public Library

30 Stroll on the Esplanade

32 Get to know the Boston Brahmin in Back Bay and Beacon Hill

23

Revisit Kennedy's Camelot

at the John F. Kennedy Presidential Library and Museum

Architecture and Historic Spots • Art and Culture • Fun for Families and Kids

Why Go: The Kennedy dynasty lives on at the John F. Kennedy Presidential Library, a sprawling complex of exhibits that tells the life story of the 35th U.S. president.

Where: The JFK Library is a 10-minute drive south of downtown Boston, or a 25-minute ride on public transportation via the Red Line subway. Take the train to the JFK/UMass station and then hop on the MBTA's 8 bus to reach the library. • Columbia Point, 617/514-1600, www.jfklibrary.org

Timing: The indoor library is open year-round, but visit in warmer months if you plan on strolling the adjoining Harborwalk while you're in the area.

In an interview at the Kennedy compound after her husband's assassination in Dallas, Jacqueline Kennedy mused to a reporter, "There will be great presidents again, but there will never be another Camelot."

President John F. Kennedy and his family have been viewed as the closest thing to an American royal family, and nowhere is it more apparent than in Boston. Members of the Kennedy clan are generally guaranteed a victory in area political races. It's hard to find a local bookshop without a Kennedy section or a university that doesn't make some claim to JFK: Boston College notes he visited the campus more often than any other university, and Harvard, which Kennedy attended, named its school of government after the late president. The University of Massachusetts system similarly has various buildings and awards named after Kennedy. To gain a better understanding of why the 35th president is so beloved by Bostonians, visit the John F. Kennedy Presidential Library.

It's hard to miss the library on Columbia Point in Boston's Dorchester neighborhood. The I.M. Pei-designed complex, notable for an imposing concrete tower and glass box atrium, is highly visible from the Southeast Expressway as well as Boston Harbor. While it may look like a cluster of separate blocks, the library is actually one big building. From inside, it can feel like

inside the JFK Presidential Library and Museum

JFK Presidential Library and Museum exterior

▲ an exhibit at the JFK Presidential Library and Museum

a typical museum, but the soaring glass atrium with a giant, dangling American flag suspended from the ceiling sets an undeniably presidential tone.

Seven permanent exhibits walk visitors through the Kennedy years: from his birthplace in Brookline, Massachusetts, to his service in World War II, to his all too brief presidency at 1600 Pennsylvania Avenue. The permanent collection includes photos, gifts from heads of state, and a replica of the Oval Office while Kennedy was in the White House. Past temporary exhibits included the audio from a 1964 interview with Jackie Kennedy shortly after her husband was assassinated. The recording was sealed until 2011 due to the sensitive nature of her real opinions on world leaders, time spent in the White House, and her widely popular reception on a 1961 state visit to France.

The library is also home to nearly all of Ernest Hemmingway's known manuscript materials, donated to the museum by his widow Mary. President Kennedy had permitted her to travel to Cuba (despite a travel ban) to claim her husband's belongings after his death in 1961.

Even if the Kennedy brand has faded in recent statewide elections (Joe Kennedy III lost in

Edward M. Kennedy Institute

The neighboring Edward M. Kennedy Institute for the United States Senate (www. em-kinstitute.org) opened in 2015 with a clear mission: to educate the public about the importance of the U.S. Senate.

In the full-scale replica of the senate chamber, visitors can engage in debate and vote on national issues, while learning how our Senate operates in a similar way.

The institute also hosts rotating art exhibits and limited history series. It's especially popular with students.

a Democratic Senate primary campaign in 2020—the first time a Kennedy lost a Massachusetts election), you can't help but feel Camelot is still alive and kicking when you set foot inside the presidential library.

Admission to the library is $14 for adults, $12 for college students with ID, and $10 for children. But most area middle and high school students visit the library at least once for school field trips. A presidential library may not seem like the most engaging activity for young ones, but the permanent exhibit on the U.S. space program and "Space Race" with Russia, as well as the Oval Office replica, are highlights for kids.

Columbia Point is quite removed from other parts of the city, but the peninsula is still a great spot to unwind after an afternoon at the library. Take time to stroll the Harborwalk and soak in the waterfront views of downtown Boston before heading back to the hustle and bustle of the city.

Connect With...

10 Go beyond Boston beer at a local distillery

27 Soak up the sun on Boston's Irish Riviera

24 Customize the Freedom Trail

Architecture and Historic Spots • Beantown Essential

Why Go: Combine stops along the popular Freedom Trail with nearby Boston gems for a dose of American History and local fun.

Where: The Freedom Trail starts at Boston Common in Beacon Hill and winds 2.5 miles through downtown Boston, into the North End, and finally ends at the Bunker Hill Monument in Charlestown.

Timing: Given that you're walking outside for the duration of the trail, I recommend enjoying it in warmer months. Spring and fall are best to avoid the peak summer tourist season. This customized Freedom Trail experience can easily be an all-day affair.

There's more than one local (and even local travel writer) who groans at the thought of the Freedom Trail, a 2.5-mile walking path along some of Boston's most important landmarks dating back to before the American Revolution. The Freedom Trail has a reputation for being lumped in with the Cheers bar and Faneuil Hall as "places only tourists go." Well, no offense to Cheers and Faneuil, but the Freedom Trail is nothing like those two. I've actually found the history-packed walking trail to be one of the most informative things I've done since moving to Boston, both in learning about my adopted hometown as well as the formation of the entire United States.

▲ Massachusetts State House

There are 16 official "stops" along the trail. Do you need to linger at all 16? Absolutely not. The must-see sites include the gold-domed Massachusetts State House, Boston Common, the Granary Burying Ground, the Old South Meeting House, the Old State House and site of the Boston Massacre, Paul Revere House, the Bunker Hill Monument, and the USS Constitution. You can still meander the entire trail from Beacon Hill to Charlestown, but focus on the high points and pair them with other local activities and sites.

I typically bypass sites that are either sandwiched by stops that need a little more time or that have changed over the years, becoming more visual attractions than places needing a lengthy tour. The Park Street Church (between the State House and the Granary Burial Ground stops), the King's Chapel and Burial Ground, the former site of the Boston Latin School (with a statue of alumni Benjamin Franklin), the site of the Old Corner Bookstore (which published American classics like Henry David Thoreau's Walden and Nathaniel Hawthorne's The Scarlet Letter but is now a Chipotle), and the Copp's Hill Burying Ground in the North End are all on this list for me—but still worth a visit if you have more time to spare!

Plan on this customized Freedom Trail walk to last about four to five hours, depending on how long you stop for snacks or tours.

Start at the **Boston Common** at Beacon Street and Park Street on Beacon Hill's southeastern border. The Common, which dates to 1634, is America's oldest public park. Puritan colonists first used it as common grazing lands for livestock, but Boston Common evolved over centuries for a variety of horrific and eventually more tranquil uses: Accused criminals and alleged witches were hanged here in the 1600s, and the Redcoats of the British military used it as a camp during the Revolutionary War. Political protests and speeches have long been part of its history, too—from 1960s Civil Rights gatherings to the Women's March of 2017. Most of the time, however, the Common is used for sunbathing and as an outdoor lunch spot near the ornate fountains on the eastern edge.

Across the Common's northern perimeter is the famed, red-brick and gold-domed **Massachusetts State House** (24 Beacon St., 617/727-3676, www.malegislature.gov). The Charles Bulfinch-designed structure has been the center of politics for the Commonwealth of Massachusetts since it opened in 1798—though, Oliver Wendall Holmes once said it was "the hub of the solar system." The gated State House complex may seem intimidating and uninviting, but visitors are welcome to take a free tour on weekdays from 10am until 3:30pm through the Secretary of the Commonwealth's office (call the office ahead of time). Tours include the House and Senate chambers, the former of which is watched over by the wooden "Sacred Cod" sculpture—an aerial reminder of the state's fishing industry.

When you've bid farewell to the Sacred Cod, walk a half block east on Beacon Street to the **Boston Athenaeum** (10-1/2 Beacon St., 617/227-0270, www.bostonathenaeum.com), which is not an official stop on the Freedom Trail but one of the oldest membership libraries in the

Paul Revere House

Old State House

Freedom Trail marker

U.S. While the library is members-only, there are free tours (approximately 1 hour) of the Athenaeum's soaring reading rooms and collections of art and British and American literature. You'll even learn about former library members like Little Women author Louisa May Alcott and President John F. Kennedy. If the tour leaves you wanting more, you can buy a day pass ($40) to work in the inspiring reading rooms or outdoor terrace.

Once you leave the Athenaeum, head east on Beacon Street, which eventually becomes School Street. Once you reach Washington Street, turn right and walk a half-block southwest to the **Old South Meeting House** (310 Washington St., 617/482-6439, www.revolutionaryspaces.org), a worthwhile stop on the trail as a gathering place for political discourse. Its historic members included the African American poet Phillis Wheatley, whose 1773 book released while she was enslaved. Benjamin Franklin was also a member. Many political debates took place here, but one of the most important involved the opposition to the British tea tax—setting the stage for the Boston Tea Party. But historic speeches didn't necessarily always mean much: The simple, white-walled sanctuary (it was also a church) with an overhead chandelier and gold-leafed eagle sculpture was put up for auction in 1872 and primed for demolition until a group of women brought in famous Bostonians like Ralph Waldo Emerson and Louisa May Alcott to save the building. The successful preservation effort is one of the earliest examples of its kind in U.S. history, and the building remains a major stop on many political campaigns, including Hillary Clinton's presidential bid in 2016.

From the meeting house, continue north on Washington until you reach the **Old State House** (206 Washington St., 617/720-1713, www.revolutionaryspaces.org). The Georgian, brick Old State House is Massachusetts' original seat of government. Today, it's a surprising pop of Revolutionary history in the middle of a bustling Financial District corner (the basement now spills into the State Street MBTA subway station). Built in 1713, the building signals its pre-Revolutionary War arrival with a golden lion and unicorn flanking the clock on the Old State House's eastern end: two symbols of the British monarchy. While you can catch the next train to Back Bay downstairs, upstairs you can take tours (every half hour, $12) led by staff in Colonial garb who give a rundown of daily life and past artifacts like the Royal Governor's chair.

The grounds of the Old State House also served as an important inflection point amid growing tension between the Colonies and Mother England that throttled the two toward battle. With tensions brewing between colonists and British troops stationed in the Massachusetts Bay colony, a group of Bostonians closed in on a British soldier on March 5, 1770. The colonists

heckled the soldier, who was eventually joined by more from the British side. The Boston side eventually escalated from words to throwing sticks and snowballs. One soldier fired his gun into the crowd, killing five and wounding six—an event the American press depicted as a massacre in the newspapers, which fueled the trajectory toward the Revolutionary War. The **Boston Massacre Site,** located on the east side of the State House, is memorialized by a medallion at the intersection of State and Congress streets.

▲ Union Square Donuts

Once you're done with the museum and massacre site, head to the **Sam Adams Taproom** (60 State St., 617/466-6418, www.samadamsbostontaproom.com), west of Faneuil Hall. While the original brewery is a train ride away on the Orange Line, the taproom is a convenient way to taste the storied local brew.

For a bite to eat, skip Faneuil's rather generic food court, and walk a block north for another off-Freedom Trail stop on Congress Street: the **Boston Public Market** (100 Hanover St., 617/973-4909, www.bostonpublicmarket.com). This popular food hall includes 30 artisans and food vendors under one roof, including stalls from popular local eateries like Bon Me, George Howell Coffee, and Union Square Donuts. Alternatively, you can cross the **Rose Kennedy Greenway** into the North End for one of many Italian lunch spots on Hanover Street.

Once you're well-fed, you'll be ready to make the trek to the **Paul Revere House** (19 N. Square, 617/523-2338, www.paulreverehouse.org) named for its resident who famously alerted Revolutionaries of Red Coat troop movement ("one if by land, two if by sea"). This small gray home, built in 1680 on a cobblestone square in the North End, was Revere's home at the start of the Revolutionary War. One of the first historic home museums when it opened in 1908 to the public, the Paul Revere House features $5 tours that encompass Revere's work both before and after the Revolution.

From Paul Revere House, head out to Charlestown to find the **Bunker Hill Monument** (Monument Sq., Charlestown, 617/242-5641, www.nps.gov), a granite obelisk commemorating the bloody Battle of Bunker Hill, where Revolutionaries clashed with the British army.

Southeast of the monument is the last stop on the trail: the **USS *Constitution* Museum** (Building 22, Charlestown Navy Yard, Charlestown, 617/426-1812, www.ussconstitutionmuseum.org). The *Constitution* launched in 1797 as one of the original six ships commissioned for the then-infant United States Navy. Better known as "Old Ironsides," the wood-hulled ship got her reputation after defeating five British warships and repelling enemy fire during a battle in the War of 1812. Some questioned if it was really just wood that comprised the *Constitution*'s hull, with a British soldier reportedly yelling during the battle, "...her sides are made of iron!" after watching cannonballs bounce off the ship's side. The *Constitution*'s popularity spared her from the scrapyard over the centuries, and she is the oldest commissioned vessel in the world. The museum includes an interactive exhibit portraying life at sea during the ship's battles, as well as vessel history and depictions of what life was like in early America.

If you're unfamiliar with the area it can be a little difficult to figure out how to get back to the city from here. Don't waste this waterfront opportunity on an Uber! You can hop aboard a water taxi from the Charlestown Navy Yard and cruise back downtown or to Seaport to enjoy skyline views and a sunset after a comprehensive lesson on American (and Boston) history.

Connect With...

14 Meander the Rose Kennedy Greenway
25 Eat Italian food on Hanover Street
32 Get to know the Boston Brahmin in Back Bay and Beacon Hill

25 Eat Italian food on Hanover Street

Drink and Dine • Beantown Essential • Neighborhoods and City Streets

Why Go: Boston has more cooking in the kitchen than just lobster rolls and clam chowder. Dining at one of the delicious Italian eateries on Hanover Street in the North End never disappoints.

Where: The North End and Hanover Street are across the Rose Kennedy Greenway and directly to the northeast of Government Center and downtown Boston. The easiest way to get to the North End is via the Orange Line to Haymarket Station followed by a five-minute walk across the Greenway to Hanover Street.

Timing: Hearty pastas and red wine are best enjoyed on a cold winter night. But crisp pizzas and an after-dinner cannoli are just as delectable in the dog days of summer. In short, there's never a bad time to venture to the North End.

When the moon hits your eye like a big pizza pie, that's—ok, I'll stop. Boston's North End is the city's equivalent of a Little Italy, and Hanover Street is the main thoroughfare of *panetterias*, and kitchens that dole out red sauce and a litany of carb-a-licious Italian dishes. Hanover Street only runs about six blocks off the Rose Kennedy Greenway, but this stretch packs a punch with some of the biggest names in Italian cuisine in the entire city.

It can be a little overwhelming trying to decide which restaurant to pick. Lined with eateries on either side, the congested thoroughfare is usually bustling with tourists walking the Freedom Trail and local Bostonians craving a carb-laden meal. But one of the best things about the North End is it is largely devoid of chain establishments, so even the take-out pizza shops are authentic. The biggest factor in choosing a place to eat is deciding how crowded you want your dining experience to be. As a general rule, restaurants are less noisy and packed the further you walk away from Cross Street and the Kennedy Greenway.

Strega (379 Hanover St., 617/523-8481, www.stregabynickvarano.com) and **Bricco** (241 Hanover St., 617/248-6800, www.bricco.com) make frequent appearances in celebrity gossip columns for attracting stars in town while filming big budget Hollywood features. These venues, owned by longtime neighborhood restaurateurs Nick Varano and Frank DePasquale, re-

▲ cannoli

▲ spaghetti dinner

▲ Boston's Italian North End

spectively, are quintessential Hanover Street in sleek, dimly lit dining rooms serving a variety of Italian staples. Steaks at both restaurants will lead to eye-popping bills (perhaps save those for special occasions), while pastas are more affordable and, dare I say, the most impressive part of either menu. It's especially difficult to snag a reservation at Strega, so call about a week ahead to ensure a table.

Lucia Ristorante (415 Hanover St., 617/367-2353, www.luciab.st) and **Carmelina's** (307 Hanover St., 617/742-0020, www.carmelinasboston.com) aren't talked about as much as Strega and Bricco, but that's ideal for a local in pursuit of a great meal without a long wait. Both restaurants offer delicious Italian dishes, generally affordable wine lists, and close proximity to the Paul Revere House—satisfy both your hunger and your quest for Revolutionary history! About two blocks north of Strega, Lucia has been doling out its extensive menu of pastas and Italian takes on meats and fish since 1977. Carmelina's offers a more modern dining experience, with an open kitchen layout where diners can watch their meals being prepared.

My all-time favorite is **Pomodoro** (351 Hanover St., 617/367-4348). Two words: chicken carbonara. I'm not even that crazy about creamy sauces, but this is my one exception. The salty, crispy bacon mixed with creamy parmesan sauce and juicy bits of chicken is just the perfect combination I keep returning to (along with my gym the morning after). Everything about the dining room here screams special occasion: wine bottles line shelves along the perimeter, accented by the occasional flickering candle. Waiters are known to often dole out an extra helping of an appetizer or pour of wine. But fear not: I've been known to come here on dates with myself (yes, the carbonara is that good).

Of course, entrees are just one part of the excitement of Hanover Street. For a true taste of Italy, you must end every dinner with cannoli at one (or both) of the North End's famous rival bakeries.

Modern Pastry (257 Hanover St., 617/523-3783, www.modernpastry.com) and **Mike's Pastry** (300 Hanover St., 617/742-3050, www.mikespastry.com) both lay claim to having the best cannoli in town, and both bakeries pre-date many of the restaurants on Hanover Street. Modern Pastry opened in 1930 and has expanded only twice in its lifetime to accommodate the constantly growing line of people down the street jostling to get in for a variety of cannoli, tira-

Origins: The North End

Boston's North End was always a popular neighborhood with new immigrants due to its proximity to the waterfront and historic shipping terminals. But it was also a melting pot where wealthy families lived among working-class groups before the American Revolution.

Eventually, the neighborhood became crowded with commercial development, and wealthier residents moved to neighborhoods like Beacon Hill. Irish immigrants were the first to the neighborhood, but by the late 1800s it became mostly populated with Jewish and Italian immigrants. The original wave of Italian immigrants came from Genoa in Northern Italy and were later joined by Southern Italians like the Campanians, Sicilians, Neapolitans, and other groups who all took their own chunks of the neighborhood. North Square even took on the name of Little Italy, and by 1930 the population was almost entirely Italian. Italian bakeries, restaurants, shops, and services poured into the neighborhood as a result.

While the North End of today is decidedly more diverse, the Italian legacy lives on within the commercial stretch of Hanover Street—especially in the kitchen.

misu, and other Italian treats. A block to the north, Mike's opened in 1946 and similarly draws enormous crowds out the door for boxes of post-dinner treats.

There are ardent defenders of each venue, as they both have an impressive variety of cannoli flavors like Oreo, hazelnut, and basic ricotta. The biggest difference is Modern fills the cannoli with ricotta on the spot while Mike's are pre-filled and ready to pack up from the case. I'm always more than happy to taste test both—who doesn't love extra dessert? If you're too full for dessert after eating a plateful of pasta, keep in mind cannoli are an excellent breakfast substitute the morning after a night in the North End.

Connect With...

① Root for the home team
⑭ Meander the Rose Kennedy Greenway
㉔ Customize the Freedom Trail

26 Explore Fenway beyond the Red Sox

Neighborhoods and City Streets

Why Go: Everyone knows Boston's Fenway neighborhood is home to the great cathedral of American sports: Fenway Park. But this stretch of the city has also turned into one of the region's hottest neighborhoods for food, housing, industry, and culture.

Where: "The Fenway" is to the west of Back Bay and accessed by the MBTA Green Line subway, getting off either at Kenmore Station on the B, C, or D lines, or at Fenway Station on the D Line. The neighborhood's borders are roughly defined by the Charlesgate roadway to the east, Park Drive to the south and west, and Beacon Street and the Massachusetts Turnpike to the north.

Timing: Summer is the most popular time of year to visit the neighborhood, during baseball season. However, more year-round attractions like Time Out Market Boston, the House of Blues music venue, and the Trillium Brewing Co. Fenway taproom make it ideal to visit in any season.

No matter your sports allegiance, the word "Fenway" likely conjures up the crack of a baseball bat, a soaring baseball, and the roar of the crowd after a home run. But the surrounding Fenway neighborhood has blossomed into more than a destination for sports fans, becoming an under-the-radar enclave for new housing, trendy eateries, and tech and life science professionals. There were talks of tearing down the ballpark in the 1990s and replacing it with something new, but luckily new ownership and city leaders held onto America's most iconic ballpark and built a thriving neighborhood beyond the Green Monster.

First, let's clear up a common misconception: The Fenway name belongs to the neighborhood—not the ballpark. The area got its moniker from the Fenway parkway, designed by Frederick Law Olmstead as part of his Emerald Necklace network of parks running around the "neck" of the Boston peninsula. The **Back Bay Fens** (100 Park Dr., 617/635-4505), better known as "The Fens," is part of the Emerald Necklace and passes through Fenway, featuring walking and running trails, footbridges over the Muddy River, a rose garden, and a variety of memorials, including one to "America the Beautiful" songwriter Katharine Lee Bates near the Museum of Fine Arts.

Despite the origin of the neighborhood's name, the stadium gives the area most of its reputation. "When they raze Fenway, it'll be like cutting down an old tree. Count the rings. There's one for each celebration and heartache suffered by Red Sox fans," *Boston Globe* sports columnist Dan Shaughnessy wrote in his book *Fenway: A Biography in Words and Pictures*. Fenway Park arrived in 1912, and it is still the most iconic piece of architecture in the area, though these days it is increasingly dwarfed by glass condo and apartment towers, an array of shops, and restaurants from some of Boston's celebrity chefs.

Originally viewed as a pass-through neighborhood of parking lots between the ballpark and nearby Longwood Medical Center, the Fenway boomed as developers looked to tap into Boston's growing life science sector. With that change came a growth in the neighborhood's dining scene, which shifted from ballpark fare to imaginative culinary creations from local master chefs. Chef Tiffani Faison has built an empire of Fenway restaurants, from the barbecue

▲ Back Bay Fens

at **Sweet Cheeks Q** (1381 Boylston St., 617/266-1300, www.sweetcheeksq.com) to Southeast Asian down the block at **Tiger Mama** (1363 Boylston St., 617/425-6262, www.tigermamaboston.com) and the "adult snack bar" of **Fool's Errand** (1377 Boylston St., www.foolserrandboston.com). Over at the **Time Out Market Boston** (401 Park Dr., 978/393-8088, www.timeout.com), one of Boston's bustling food halls, you can sample some of the city's best bites: meatballs from James Beard Award winner Michael Schlow, the Craigie burger from chef Tony Maws (who helms Craigie on Main across the river in Cambridge), and nori tacos from renowned chef Tim Cushman. It's nearly impossible to pick just one spot to dine, so take your time and try them all!

If you're craving art and culture while in the neighborhood, check out the **Isabella Stewart Gardner Museum** (25 Evans Way, 617/566-1401, www.gardnermuseum.org) along the southwest corner of the Fens, where you can learn about the famous art heist that took place in one of the galleries. Or stop by the impressive **Museum of Fine Arts** (465 Hunting-

▲ Time Out Market Boston

ton Ave., 617/267-9300, www.mfa.org), which contains over 450,000 pieces of art, including a wide variety of American art.

When you're ready to imbibe, stop by **Trillium Brewing Co. Fenway** in Time Out Market. Relax in the beer garden with a refreshing pale ale, like Mosaic Fort Point, or a creative IPA/wine combo, like the Dialed Down Sauvignon Blanc. **Nathálie** (186 Brookline Ave., 857/317-3884, www.nathaliebar.com) is also a great option. The chic wine bar serves a wide variety of interesting wines (grouped by headings like "cheeky & fresh," and "fiery") with tasty food pairings.

Once you've explored the neighborhood, from the verdant Fens to the hip and delicious restaurants, you'll be convinced that it's more than just the ballpark. That said, a **Fenway Park Tour** (https://www.mlb.com/redsox/ballpark/tours, $21) is still a wonderful way to spend your time, no matter if you've lived in Boston for over a decade or you just moved up for college last week.

Connect With...

1 Root for the home team

3 Sleuth the unsolved art heist at the Isabella Stewart Gardner Museum

20 Kayak the Charles River

27 Soak up the sun on Boston's Irish Riviera

On the Water • Get Outside

Why Go: Sure, places like Cape Cod or Nantucket may have the region's sun-soaked stunners when it comes to beaches, but when you're looking to just get a good base tan and relax with friends, the South Boston beaches along William J Day Boulevard are an easy way to get some sand between the toes before heading to nearby Southie bars once the sun goes down.

Where: The stretch of M Street Beach to Castle Island is along South Boston's southern and eastern borders. Massachusetts Bay Transit Authority buses like the 11 and 7 all run to the beach. • 617/727-5290, https://www.mass.gov/locations/castle-island-pleasure-bay-m-street-beach-and-carson-beach

Timing: Summer months are the best time to go to the beach, but Sullivan's snack shack is known to open in late February to provide an early taste of the warm months to come for those looking to stroll Castle Island during colder parts of the year.

Places like M Street Beach and Castle Island have a reputation for being Boston's Irish Riviera due to their proximity to the historically Irish enclave of South Boston, where today there is still a heavy Irish presence (or at least people who claim Irish descent) along with a swelling mix of young professionals.

The sandy stretch of urban bliss along William J Day Boulevard is a meeting place for Boston's diverse population: members of the LGBTQ+, Black, and Latinx communities along with preppy post-grads, Southie bros, and others all converge here to catch some rays and bathe in the summer heat. But it hasn't always been that way. The neighborhood's grittier past and proximity to Boston Logan International Airport made it pretty undesirable. However, real estate is a hot commodity throughout all of Beantown these days, and beaches in this part of town increasingly look less like the Southie of your favorite mafia movie and more like a pool party in Las Vegas—well, if that party in Vegas had jets flying overhead and the occasional state trooper checking for overt instances of public drinking. (It isn't legally allowed, but...show me a Yeti cooler on the beach that isn't stocked with Bud Light and lunch is on me.)

▲ strolling along the water at the beach

▲ one of South Boston's beaches

Make no mistake: the beaches of Boston's Irish Riviera aren't exactly like the romantic and glamorous coastlines of Nice or Croatia—but they offer the residents a great way to see and be seen in the summer months.

Midway down M Street Beach (and usually the source of blaring club hits) is **Kiki Beach,** a name given to the place where many LGBTQ+ sunbathers hang out on Saturdays in the summer. Short bathing suits and chiseled abs are standard in this part of the Irish Riviera—though I possess neither and still have a great time alternating between bronzing and a quick dip in Boston Harbor. Be sure to grab picnic supplies at nearby cafes or markets like **American Provisions** (613 E Broadway, 617-269-6100, www.americanprovisions.com) ahead of your trip.

Further east from M Street and Kiki Beach is the more family-friendly **Castle Island.** The so-called island, actually a peninsula on the easternmost edge of Southie, is home to walking trails, the historic **Fort Independence** (2010 William J Day Blvd.) that dates to 1833, and most importantly (to me, anyway), **Sullivan's** (2080 William J Day Blvd., 617/268-5685, www. sullivanscastleisland.com). Sullivan's— better known as Sully's—is a classic snack shack, but

Fort Independence

in 1951, serving fried seafood and hot dogs, perfect for a sweltering day at a city beach. Grab a bite and take it around to the eastern edge of Castle Island to enjoy lunch with a waterfront view.

Even if you are more inclined to visit Cape Cod or Nantucket, a Boston beach is still worth a visit for those weekends when you just don't have the time (or patience) to sit in traffic. Might I once again mention the fried food at Sully's? OK, fine, the sunbathing is nice, too.

Connect With...

1. Go beyond Boston beer at a local distillery
2. Escape to the Boston Harbor Islands
4. Try your luck at New England casinos

28 Go to a concert

Boston Parties • Art and Culture

Why Go: Whether you're looking for an intimate show on a small stage or an arena-sized blowout with the biggest name du jour, Boston has an array of live music venues perfect for all tastes.

Where: Boston's live music venues are scattered across the city and into Cambridge. The neighborhoods with the highest concentration of concert halls or venues include Downtown, the Seaport, Fenway, and Allston/Brighton.

Timing: Most of these venues are indoors, so there isn't a bad time of year to attend a performance. However, some outdoor venues in the Seaport only offer performances in the summer.

From the kind of place that thrives on sweaty mosh pits to more refined performing arts centers, Boston has a little bit of everything. Music acts like Aerosmith, the Pixies, the Dropkick Murphys, and Boston (duh) all got their start here. Even U2 got their break after the old local rock radio station WBCN started playing the Irish group. So, it's only natural that such a musical city would have all types of venues for bands, old and new, big and small, to perform.

The biggest names in music, like Taylor Swift and John Mayer, typically perform at huge venues with tens of thousands of seats like the **TD Garden** (100 Legends Way, 617/624-1000, www.tdgarden.com) downtown or **Gillette Stadium** (1 Patriot Pl., Foxborough, 508/543-8200, www.gillettestadium.com). **Fenway Park** (4 Jersey St., 877/733-7699, www.mlb.com), home of the Red Sox, even hosts concerts for groups like the Dave Matthews Band or Phish in the summer. Pay careful attention to seating charts when you buy tickets for shows at venues like the Garden or Gillette, which can place fans in nosebleed sections or, even worse, seats behind the stage! (Obviously, that's not ideal.)

Leader Bank Pavilion (290 Northern Ave., 617/728-1600, www.livenation.com) is a personal favorite of mine. This waterfront concert venue is located on the eastern half of Seaport near the **Harpoon Brewery** (306 Northern Ave., 617/456-2322, www.harpoonbrewery.

House of Blues Boston

com), which is perfect for a pre-performance libation. The outdoor amphitheater hosts major names like Diana Ross, Lauryn Hill, and Radiohead with amazing views of Boston Harbor beyond the stage. With just over 5,000 seats, the Pavilion is a larger venue, but small enough to give all attendees a pretty good view of the performance.

There are other interesting venues of all sizes throughout the city. **Paradise Rock Club** (967 Commonwealth Ave., 617/562-8800, www.crossroadspresents.com) and **Brighton Music Hall** (158 Brighton Ave., Allston, 617/779-0141, www.crossroadspresents.com) in the Allston/Brighton neighborhoods typically feature local rock acts as well as touring artists just beginning to inch their way up the Billboard music charts. These venues all host less than 1,000 people in intimate settings where basically every concertgoer is steps away from the lead singer, and everyone is sweaty trying to get as close to the stage as possible.

House of Blues Boston (15 Lansdowne St., 888/693-2583, www.houseofblues.com) behind Fenway Park is one of 11 House of Blues locations in the United States. It sees an eclectic mix of touring artists, as the venue can handle several thousand fans for acts looking for something slightly more intimate than TD Garden but also aware they can fill up something bigger than the Paradise Rock Club. The House of Blues certainly exudes cool, with its bohemian look and art-adorned walls. The variety of bars across two floors are within the concert hall, so it's impossible to miss your favorite song while you're getting a beverage during Kelly Clarkson's or Niall Horan's encore. Most of the venue is standing-room-only, but there is limited seating on the upper two levels.

In the Greater Boston area, across the Charles River in Cambridge, venues like **The Sinclair** (52 Church St., Cambridge, 617/547-5200, www.sinclaircambridge.com) in Harvard Square and the **Middle East** (472-480 Massachusetts Ave., Cambridge, 617/864-3278, www.mideastoffers.com) in Central Square are two popular spots to catch a concert. The Middle East is a sprawling complex of different venues, from night clubs to hip hop clubs and even belly dancing. The Sinclair is even more eclectic, hosting everything from emo cover band nights to Jessie Ware. It is also newer, with some seating available in the back. The Middle East is an older institution; therefore, it also has its grimier elements, with standing-room only spaces

▲ Gillette Stadium

that feel more like seeing a performance in someone's basement due to exposed pipes and low ceiling heights. Both venues have full bars.

Ticket prices for each of these venues vary, from $10 or $15 shows at places like the Sinclair and the Middle East to pricier headliners at the TD Garden and Gillette Stadium that soar well over $100. The other venues generally fall somewhere in the middle. Places are very strict about bringing in outside food and drink, so plan to buy at the venues. Apart from Gillette, which has a sprawling parking lot (but insane traffic), parking is limited, so take advantage of public transit and save yourself some potential road rage.

Connect With...

26 Explore Fenway beyond the Red Sox
36 Go beyond Harvard Yard in Cambridge and Somerville

29 Brunch around the World
in the South End

Neighborhoods and City Streets • Drink and Dine

Why Go: There are countless brunch options all over the city, but the South End is my favorite because it serves as a lesser-known meeting place for a wide range of cultures, providing an opportunity for visitors to sample different cuisines in a neighborhood beloved by locals.

Where: The South End is directly south of Back Bay and west of South Boston. The easiest way to get to the neighborhood is to take the Orange Line to Back Bay and walk south on Dartmouth Street. Other options include taking the Silver Line, which skirts the neighborhood's southern edge along Washington Street.

Timing: There's no bad time to brunch here. Summer months include more outdoor seating while colder months are great for cozy tables at places like Aquitaine.

The unofficial weekend sport in Boston's diverse, brick-paved South End neighborhood is brunching. I've lived in the South End since 2011 and have tried every brunch spot at least ten times. (My credit card statement never lies. Ouch.) Some good ones have come and gone; some not-so-good ones have somehow managed to stick around. But I can point you in the direction of restaurants and parts of the neighborhood worth your time.

It might come as a surprise how varied South End kitchens are, given the painstaking process neighborhood groups have taken to keep the area's collective identity rooted in brick, Victorian rowhouses. But never judge a book (or restaurant) by its cover—beneath the homogenous Victorian façade are delectable creations from around the world. The blend of Puerto Rican, Syrian, Greek, and Indian communities across Greater Boston converge here with some of the city's best dining rooms.

Villa Victoria, in the heart of the South End on Tremont Street, is a historically affordable housing development with a significant Puerto Rican population. The South End benefits from the Puerto Rican cultural influence on the neighborhood, and that's especially true for diners at **Vejigantes Restaurant** (57 W Dedham St., 617/247-9249, www.vejigantesrestaurant.com). With bright décor and a robust menu, this women-led restaurant doesn't disappoint. The pael-

South End brownstones

Shawmut Avenue

B&G Oysters

las (especially the lobster, shrimp, calamari, and clam variety) and *churrasco con salsa chimich-urri* (grilled beef with chimichurri sauce), are some of my favorite dishes.

Nearby at **Aquitaine** (569 Tremont St., 617/424-8577, www.aquitaineboston.com), brunch-goers enjoy French cuisine in a warm, bistro-style space. Classic brunch cocktails like Bloody Marys and Bellinis pair well with hearty dishes like the confit duck hash and eggs or the truffle asparagus omelet.

Across the street is **Frenchie Wine Bistro** (560 Tremont St., 857/233-5941, www.frenchieboston.com). Aquitaine's direct competitor, Frenchie also servers French fare (as the name suggests), but the two restaurant menus are different enough that you should visit both at some point. Frenchie offers a large wine list and tasty dishes (try the charcuterie, the oysters of the day, or *eggs a la provencale*) in a beautiful space with floral accents.

For delicious Greek food and wine, stop by **Kava neo-taverna** (315 Shawmut Ave., 617/356-1100, www.kavaneotaverna.com). Order several small plates like the imam (eggplant stuffed with tomato, onion, garlic, and kasseri cheese), *kolokithakia* (zucchini chips with tzatziki), or *saganaki garides* (baked shrimp with peppers, onion, tomatoes, and feta), and watch the world go by from their beautiful outdoor patio space.

At **Mela** (578 Tremont St., 617/859-4805, www.melaboston.com), you'll find authentic Indian cuisine cooked to perfection. The large menu, with popular items like vegetable samosas, chicken tikka masala, and garlic naan, guarantees diners won't leave hungry. The warmth of the space is matched by the service. Don't skip the mango mimosas.

Other great venues in the neighborhood are also among some of the city's most popular dining options. **B&G Oysters** (550 Tremont St., 617/423-0550, www.bandgoysters.com) from celebrity chef Barbara Lynch, has a great raw bar, as well as New England classics like lobster rolls and fried oysters, all of which are best enjoyed on the cozy patio.

From former Barbara Lynch protégé Colin Lynch (no relation) is **Bar Mezzana** (360 Harrison Ave., 617/530-1770, www.barmezzana.com). Dreamy Italian pasta dishes like bucatini carbonara and cacio e pepe sit side by side on the menu with lighter options like brioche toast with whipped butter, and brunch classics like the egg sandwich. Humorously named cocktails like "orange you glad I didn't say mimosa" and "everything but the bloody" pair nicely with just about anything.

The South End's Legacy of Diversity

In the late 1800s, landfill projects created new neighborhoods, like Back Bay to the North, which encouraged some residents of the South End to move out and others to move in. Victorian single-family rowhouses were divided and transformed into affordable housing, and diverse groups of immigrants, Black railroad workers, and gay men dominated the neighborhood throughout the 1900s.

Overwhelming pushback on Boston's urban renewal plans in the 1950s saved much of the neighborhood's original architecture, but areas closest to Chinatown were still bulldozed. However, the urban planning fight ultimately sparked the preservation and creation of affordable housing with historically diverse populations like Villa Victoria and Castle Square, home to a large population of Chinese Americans.

The South End is still (proudly) one of the most diverse neighborhoods in Boston.

Toro (1704 Washington St., 617/536-4300, www.toro-restaurant.com), a little out of the way from the other restaurants, is a super popular tapas spot that has gone global with locations in Dubai and New York City. With meaty fare like *filete a la plancha* (hangar steak with romesco) and *asado de huesos* (roasted bone marrow), and vegetarian dishes like *tortilla Española* (egg and potato omelet) and maíz asado (grilled corn with aioli, lime, and cheese), Toro has options for a variety of diners. The cocktail list is also great.

As brunch veterans know, brunch can last for hours. So don't worry if you show up around lunchtime; you'll still have a chance to enjoy this in-between weekend meal with a cocktail or two. Be warned: one too many mimosas can lead to dangerous shopping splurges at the many nearby boutique stores.

Connect With...

5 Marvel at the Boston Public Library
7 Soak in sequin overload at a Jacques' drag show
17 Gallery hop in SoWA

30 Stroll on the Esplanade

Get Outside • Fun for Families and Kids

Why Go: Boston is known for being a pretty green city with many parks, but the Charles River Esplanade is one-of-a-kind when it comes to its running trails, waterfront docks, and skyline views.

Where: The Esplanade runs along the Charles River's south bank along Back Bay's northern border. It is accessible by footbridges across Storrow Drive, with the bridges at Massachusetts Avenue, Dartmouth Street, and Arlington Street the easiest to access. • 617/227-0365, https://esplanade.org

Timing: The Esplanade is open year-round, and runners training for the Boston Marathon are known to frequent it even after a snowstorm. But warmer months are generally the most popular, especially for events like the 4th of July fireworks or even pop-up beer gardens.

The nearby Boston Common and the Boston Public Garden may get more tourist love when it comes to city greenspaces, but the Charles River Esplanade is a favorite among active locals—and it's not hard to see why. Whether you're training for the Boston Marathon, taking advantage of the **Paul Dudley White Bike Path,** enjoying an outdoor yoga class, or, like me, you're just trying to get in a quick burst of cardio before stopping at one of the delicious bakeries along nearby Newbury Street to cancel out that exercise (I kid...sort of), the Charles River Esplanade offers miles of paved, picturesque paths and sweeping lawns.

In addition to popular outdoor recreation opportunities, this three-mile stretch along the Charles River between the Museum of Science and the Boston University Bridge plays an important role as a meeting place for Bostonians. Stop by the **docks** to enjoy a picnic overlooking the water. Take little ones to any of the three playgrounds: the **Esplanade Playspace, Stoneman Playground,** or **Charlesbank Playground** for climbing, swinging, sliding, and zip-lining. Visit **Hatch Memorial Shell** for special events like the 4th of July concert (with fireworks) performed by the Boston Pops Orchestra. Relax with a brew in a **pop-up beer**

▲ boats on the Charles River

▲ chilling out on the Esplanade

▲ one of the Esplanade's floating docks

garden for local breweries like Night Shift. Or simply stroll along the path, keeping an eye out for **colorful murals.**

The wonderful thing about the Esplanade is its location, stretching behind several neighborhoods—which makes it easy to customize your trips and have new experiences every time. My perfect Esplanade experience involves grabbing a book from the **Boston Public Library** (700 Boylston St., 617/536-5400, www.bpl.org) in Copley Square or one of the independent bookshops like **Trident Booksellers** (338 Newbury St., 617/267-8688, www.tridentbookscafe.com), then perusing a small café or market nearby for a snack (Oh, who are we kidding? A full meal) before heading over to the Esplanade for an afternoon of reading and relaxation on a waterfront dock. I also never tire of the cityscape views. The Cambridge, Back Bay, and downtown Boston skylines are all visible from the trail.

It's best to walk to the Esplanade; parking options are generally non-existent and public transportation options, like the Charles/MGH stop on the Red Line subway or Copley and Arlington stations on the Green Line are located conveniently nearby. Restrooms as well as snack

▲ a running trail on the Esplanade

Storrow Drive

The Esplanade is increasingly used as a rallying cry for Boston to move away from car culture, particularly due to an early benefactor. Helen Osborne Storrow donated $1 million in the early 1900s that cleared the way for many improvements to the park, including lagoons, boat landings, and playgrounds. While Storrow's donation expanded and improved the Esplanade, a roadway project in the 1950s severely cut off the Esplanade from Back Bay. That road, Storrow Drive, was later named after Helen—despite her objections to such roadway expansion.

options and beer gardens are generally open from spring through fall—so plan ahead for visits in colder months.

Connect With...

⑤ Marvel at the Boston Public Library

⑳ Kayak the Charles River

㉜ Get to know the Boston Brahmin in Back Bay and Beacon Hill

31 Go on a TV- and movie-themed pub crawl

Drink and Dine • Boston Parties

Why Go: The Boston TV and movie crawl takes you through all facets of city living. L Street Tavern and Murphy's Law offer hefty pours of South Boston's Irish roots in a neighborhood that's in danger of losing its historic identity. Closer to Beacon Hill, Mooo... and No. 9 Park are real-life backdrops to what would have been the stomping grounds of power attorneys on *Ally McBeal*.

Where: Start in Harvard Square at Grendel's Den. Take the Red Line subway to the Harvard MBTA station and walk out of the main exit of the station onto Massachusetts Avenue. Turn south on John F. Kennedy St. and go two blocks to Winthrop Square, where Grendel's is on the southwest corner of the tiny park.

Timing: There's no bad time of year to visit L Street, but St. Patrick's Day can be both a blessing and a curse: long-time residents show up in droves...but so do people who only come one time a year, and that can lead to rowdiness in bars and displeased looks from full-time residents. Murphy's Law can get picky on who can come in late at night on Fridays and Saturdays (don't try unless you live nearby and know the bouncer). Grendel's Den is busiest around sporting events like the Head of the Charles Regatta in October and Harvard football games in the fall. Other stops on this pub crawl are fine at all times of year; however, Cheers is usually always packed with tourists.

Beantown has been a fixture on everything from '80s/'90s television hits like *Cheers* and *Ally McBeal* to Academy Award-winning films like *Good Will Hunting* and *The Departed*. Sure, many

"Boston" film sets are actually replicas built in Hollywood, but some of the locations, and the inspiration for the replicas, are still around today. Therefore, it is my duty to show you how to explore Boston TV and movie history with a pub crawl through Harvard Square and into the heart of Boston.

Start the pub crawl at one of the most popular bars in Harvard Square, **Grendel's Den** (89 Winthrop St., 617/491-1160, www.grendelsden.com). While it may get its name from the man-devouring monster from Beowulf, Grendel's restaurant is known for serving up smooth

▲ Church of the Covenant

Grendel's Den

film memorabilia at L Street Tavern

inside Grendel's Den

cocktails, local beer, and casual bar food like spinach pie and roast beef sandwiches. Ben Affleck's reported affinity for Grendel's led to its cameo as a lunch spot in *The Town*, which he directed (and also appeared in with co-stars Rebecca Hall and Jeremy Renner). While the on-screen scene is a little tense, with Renner's character nearly revealing details about the film's initial bank robbery, fret not: usually the most raucous the bar gets in real life is on a weekend night with college students.

Once you've wrapped at Grendel's, head to the nearby Harvard MBTA station on the Red Line and take an inbound subway four stops (about a 15-minute ride) to Park Street. From the station head northwest one block on Park Street to the **Massachusetts State House** (24 Beacon St., 617/722-2000, www.malegislature.gov). Stop and admire the gold-domed building and recall the scene in *The Departed* when Matt Damon's character sat on a park bench outside, full of dark ambition, or—*spoiler alert*—the final scene where a rat can be seen scampering by the windowsill of his posh apartment overlooking the state house (an obvious analogy for his two-timing ways with the mob).

From the state house, head two buildings east on Beacon Street to the **American Congregational Association building** (14 Beacon St. #100, 617/523-0604, www.congregationallibrary.org). Nineties TV aficionados will recognize this exterior as the home of the fictional law firm Cage and Fish in *Ally McBeal*. Fans will be disappointed to find the bar featured at the end of each episode (and often featuring cameos from the likes of Barry Manilow, Elton John, and Mariah Carey) doesn't actually exist in the lobby. But the American Congregational Association building is still worth a stop, and there are plenty of nearby places to grab a drink fit for a power attorney. **Mooo...** (15 Beacon St., 617/670-2515, www.mooorestaurant.com), across the street, is one of Boston's high-end steakhouses, but its sleek bar with dark décor and soft lighting is a romantic spot for a glass of wine or clandestine cocktail.

The next stop is less high-end and usually packed with tourists. Walk about a half-mile, or four-ish blocks, west on Beacon Street from Mooo... to **Cheers** (84 Beacon St., 617/227-9605, www.cheersboston.com), the bar made globally famous by the TV show of the same name. While this venue is almost more popular as a gift shop than it is a bar, and locals tend to roll

Murphy's Law

inside Cheers

the iconic Cheers sign

their eyes at the mere mention of its name, it is still fun to grab a pint of a locally brewed Harpoon IPA inside, just to say you've been to the place "where everybody knows your name."

From Cheers, walk around the northwest perimeter of the Boston Public Garden along Beacon Street and onto Arlington, then finally a block west on Newbury Street to get to the **Church of the Covenant** (67 Newbury St., 617/266-7480, www.cotcbos.org), featured early in *The Boondock Saints* as the setting where the MacManus brothers (played by Sean Patrick Flanery and Norman Reedus) attend Mass. While you won't find McGinty's, their preferred on-film watering hole, you can grab a drink nearby at **Street Bar** at the **Newbury Boston** (1 Newbury St., 617/536-5700, www.thenewburyboston.com), one of the city's finest hotels.

To make the most of your time, grab an Uber or Lyft to **Murphy's Law** (837 Summer St., 617/269-6667, www.murphyslawbar.com). It's usually a $10-15 ride for this 12-minute trip (you can technically take the #9 bus from Berkeley and Boylston Streets on the MBTA network, but that is a more time-consuming—albeit cheaper—option). The bar, a "locals only" kind of place in the later hours of a weekend night, was used as a stand-in for a watering hole-turned-shootout in the Ben Affleck-directed *Gone Baby Gone*. Grab a Sam Adams, chat with the friendly bartenders or owner Kathy Murphy, and then head out to your next stop. Note: Murphy's Law can get rather rowdy the later you stay.

To close out the pub crawl, walk eight blocks south on Summer Street (which eventually turns into L Street) to where it intersects with 8th Street in the heart of South Boston (aka Southie). Here you'll find **L Street Tavern** (658 E 8th St.)—known as Striggy's by locals. L Street earned its place on the cinematic map due to hometown heroes Matt Damon and Ben Affleck's 1997 *film Good Will Hunting*. The bar ("Woody's" in the film) is largely where Will (Damon), Chuckie (Affleck), and their crew of Southie friends hang out. It's easy to find the tables where the movie scenes were actually filmed, as they are decked out in memorabilia that has since been lacquered over as a tabletop. But don't just gawk at silver screen history. Grab a brew like the locals do: order a pint and chase it with a shot of Dr. McGillicuddy's, a flavored liqueur, typically mint, often found on tap at many Southie bars as a popular nightcap.

Starting the pub crawl in the afternoon will give you enough time to space things out and leisurely make your way from Cambridge to Southie. Bring cash for drinks and tips, as many bars in Southie are cash-only. Beers generally range $5-8 across the city, but cocktails and wine

Cherished L Street Tavern

L Street Tavern's popularity on the national (or even global) stage comes purely from the silver screen. *Good Will Hunting* put the bar on the map, and it has become a mainstay with locals and tourists alike in the nearly 25 years since the movie came out. Ben Affleck even brought Jennifer Lopez to L Street the first time they were a couple, during the original "Bennifer" years.

But in real life, L Street goes far beyond the big screen. At a time when so much of South Boston is dictated by the highest price per square foot and increasing Starbucks storefronts (a very contentious one was begrudgingly approved a few blocks down several years ago), L Street is a much-needed slice of authentic Southie that carries on no matter the surrounding gentrification. Dark wood panels, neon bar signs, and sticky floors—you won't find that at Starbucks!

can easily surpass $15 at nicer spots like Mooo... and the Street Bar at the Newbury Boston. Southie bars will generally be your most affordable stops. A friendly reminder: Boston is a city that turns in early compared to the likes of New York City, so last call is at 2am.

Connect With...

24 Customize the Freedom Trail
36 Go Beyond Harvard Yard in Cambridge and Somerville

32 Get to know the Boston Brahmin
in Back Bay and Beacon Hill

Neighborhoods and City Streets • Architecture and Historic Spots

Why Go: Learn about the social structure driving the historic occupants of Back Bay and Beacon Hill.

Where: Back Bay and Beacon Hill are along the southern shores of the Charles River Basin, across from Cambridge. Back Bay is served directly by the Green Line MBTA subway, with stops at Hynes, Copley, and Arlington stations. The Back Bay Orange Line station is another access point. Beacon Hill is directly northeast of Back Bay, essentially perpendicular to it on the northwest corner of the Boston Public Garden. Beacon Hill is best served by the Charles/MGH Red Line subway station on the neighborhood's northern edge.

Timing: As with most parts of Boston, those averse to colder weather wouldn't want to take a leisurely stroll in either neighborhood in the winter; however, the Commonwealth Avenue Mall is lit up with holiday lights in colder months. Summer and fall are more popular times to visit.

You're probably aware that *The Mayflower* landing at Plymouth Rock put the wheels in motion for New England to eventually become what it is today, but what you may not realize is an entire social class was formed based on the occupants of the English ship, better known in history books as the Pilgrims. However, in Boston, many of the Pilgrims' descendants took on a different, lofty name based on the Hindu caste system: the **Boston Brahmin.**

Brahmins were not only wealthy, they were also meant to be virtuous, enlightened, and exude refined principles (and typically not flashy displays of wealth). This is almost certainly where Boston's stuffy reputation comes from, and why the city isn't known for late-night revelry, compared to the Big Apple three hours to the south, which "never sleeps." Founding fathers like Samuel Adams, as well as Presidents John and John Quincy Adams were Brahmins, as were the Coolidges (includ-

The Boston Public Garden connects Back Bay to Beacon Hill.

Boston skyline

townhomes in Beacon Hill

ing President Calvin Coolidge), Forbes (which counts former Secretary of State John Forbes Kerry as a member), and Winthrop families.

It's not all that uncommon to hear at least one person at a Boston dinner party make some distant claim to a Boston Brahmin family, but the city has moved on from fawning adoration of a select few family names, and instead reveres owners of local professional sports teams or pharmaceutical CEOs on the verge of a major medical breakthrough. However, it is still fun to observe vestiges of Boston's Brahmin past in **Back Bay** and **Beacon Hill.**

The stately, stone townhouses of the tree-lined **Commonwealth Avenue** include some of Boston's surviving social clubs, hubs of Brahmin activity where work was discouraged...but deals were still made. Back Bay is seen as the more "new money" (gasp) of the two neighborhoods due to it being created via a massive land filling project. Keep in mind: this land filling happened in the 1800s, but Brahmin rules are Brahmin rules!

Beacon Hill, where the more established Brahmins ruled (and some, like John Kerry, still do), provides a great opportunity to gawk at the brick Greek Revival townhomes of **Louisburg Square.** As you walk along, consider that the area was the former stomping grounds of historic figures like architect Charles Bulfinch (known for many local buildings like the gold-domed Massachusetts State House), *Atlantic* editor and author William Dean Howells, and *Little Women* author Louisa May Alcott.

Once you're done with your tour of the neighborhoods, Charles Street at the bottom of "the hill," as Beacon Hillers call it, is a great spot for shopping and eating. At **Follain** (65 Charles St., 857/233-5211, www.follain.com) treat your skin with its array of clean beauty products. **Blackstone's** (46 Charles St., 617/227-4646, www.blackstonesboston.com) offers every kitchen, home, and host or hostess gift you never knew you needed. The little shop in the heart of the Charles Street shopping district has everything from golf towels to picnic kits to Boston-themed gifts like coasters etched with historic maps of the city. Decadent restaurants can be found along the neighborhood's perimeter. **Toscano** (47 Charles St., 617/723-4090, www.toscanoboston.com) provides old-world ambience and delicious Tuscan food. Flavorful American comfort food meets cozy café style at **The Paramount** (44 Charles St., 617/720-1152, www.paramountboston.com). **No. 9 Park** (9 Park St., 617/742-9991, www.no9park.com) has a French-inspired menu in an upscale townhouse.

In Back Bay, you can live like a Brahmin and treat yourself to an ultra-luxurious cocktail at the **Newbury Boston** (1 Newbury St., 888/974-3948, www.thenewburyboston.com) or at the **Bristol Restaurant and Bar** (200 Boylston St.) at the Four Seasons Hotel Boston overlooking the Boston Public Garden.

Social clubs still exist as a quasi-reflection of how stuffy things really once were here. But that's old Boston. New Boston isn't quite as beholden to a social scene that lives and breathes by the roster of a members-only club and notable family trees. Membership is down, clubs have shuttered, and change is in the air. Boston's Brahmin lives on, rooted in the city's history, but it's good to see the shift in values around the city. Nevertheless, it can still be fun to spend a day wandering the neighborhoods where these families were once concentrated—while only having to worry about the price of a nice cocktail instead of a hefty membership fee to a social club.

Connect With...

4 Walk the Black Heritage Trail
20 Kayak the Charles River
30 Stroll on the Esplanade

33 Play at Martin's Park

Fun for Families and Kids • Get Outside

Why Go: Martin's Park is a welcoming and thoughtfully designed playground on the Fort Point Channel.

Where: Martin's Park, immediately to the south of Seaport Boulevard and north of the Boston Children's Museum, is along the eastern shore of Fort Point Channel.

Timing: Summer months are the best time to visit Martin's Park, as most nearby attractions are also enjoying their peak season.

Right on the Boston Harborwalk, the beautiful, one-acre **Martin's Park** is full of a playful array of recreation options that beckon little ones of all ages and physical abilities to let their imaginations run wild.

the play pirate ship

As you enter the park from the Harborwalk (west) side, you'll see a wooden pedestrian bridge directly in front of you. Walk toward the bridge, but veer right before you reach it to enter an area with two metal slides (with necessary shading sails positioned above them—who doesn't remember some painful sun-heated metal-slide incident from their childhood?) and a wooden amphitheater. One slide is enclosed, like a tube, and the other is open. Both sit on soft, padded ground in case some eager kiddos slide down a bit faster than they expected. Parents can watch from the conveniently positioned amphitheater, which also makes a nice spot for a snack break. (Puppet shows take place at the amphitheater, too!)

To the right of the slide area, partially hidden by trees, is a rope jungle gym. Also on padded ground (as is the rest of the playground equipment in the park), the metal and rope cosmo climber gives kids the chance to enjoy thrilling climbs in a safe space. A seat wall next to the climber gives adults a spot to sit and keep watch—and take photos of their little adrenaline junkies.

slide

rope jungle gym

Martin's Park

swings

155

Behind the rope jungle gym is an accessible path, which leads to the area at the top of the slides. As you enter the clearing with the slides, you'll see a small orange and yellow climbing hill with handholds, which leads to a log jungle gym, and a round basket swing. To the right of the basket swing, the accessible path continues to the wooden pedestrian bridge, which offers excellent views of the park, the surrounding city, and the Fort Point Channel across the Harborwalk.

After you cross the bridge, you'll reach the north side of the park, where the main attraction is a marooned ship, perfect for aspiring pirates and sea captains of all ages. Little ones can brave the bridge from the "water," or walk a flat plank from the accessible path to board the ship's deck. Inside a small wooden structure is the popular ship's wheel. South of the ship is a water garden that operates in the summer, making it a great way to cool off when the weather is warm.

There are also smaller touches scattered throughout the park: telescopes, rock scrambles, animal sculptures, interpretative signs, and talk tubes. Hundreds of trees and lots of shrubbery also make this both a much-needed spot of green in a very congested part of the city as well as a climate-resilient stretch of waterfront.

There are a variety of nearby public transportation options to get to Martin's Park, with the most convenient being **Courthouse Station** on the bus rapid transit Silver Line. This offers one-stop connections to South Station, Boston's busiest rail hub. On a nice day, it's pleasant just to get off the train or subway at South Station and walk the three blocks northeast to the park. Bike racks are available for those pedaling in from other parts of the city (bike lanes are common and convenient even through more congested parts of the neighboring Seaport and Financial District). While at the park, if nature calls (as if often does for little ones), the nearest public restroom is directly east in the office building at **51 Sleeper St.** There are also public facilities north of Seaport Blvd. at the **Envoy Hotel.**

What truly makes this park special is the feeling of inclusivity; Everyone has a place at Martin's Park. Named after Martin Richards, the youngest victim of the 2013 Boston Marathon bombing, the park follows the spirit of a child whose eight-year life was cut entirely too short. Memorials are often sad venues, but the Richards family has made this one to their son one of the most joyous, poignant parts of Greater Boston.

One Boston Day

The Boston Marathon is normally a boisterous occasion. But on April 15, 2013, the marathon was thrown into tumult with a bombing that killed three, including eight-year-old Martin Richards. A photo of Richards at school holding a sign he made saying, *No more hurting people. Peace* became a global symbol for healing from the tragedy, and work went into finding strength from such a dark day.

The city now celebrates One Boston Day each **April 15** by encouraging random acts of kindness. The Martin Richards Foundation has raised and donated millions to projects in line with values of its young namesake: kindness, peace, and generosity. Martin's Park, which was built through a variety of public and private donations, does just that by offering all children an opportunity to play in a safe, inviting place named after a very brave young man.

Connect With...

2 Go whale-watching in Boston Harbor
12 Escape to the Boston Harbor Islands
14 Meander the Rose Kennedy Greenway

34 Try your luck at New England casinos

Boston Parties

Why Go: When you think of a night on the town gambling and enjoying an all-you-can-eat buffet, your mind probably jumps to Atlantic City or Las Vegas, but you don't need to venture that far from Boston. New England has their own excellent casinos for anyone trying to hit the jackpot.

Where: Mohegan Sun, 1 Mohegan Sun Blvd., Uncasville, CT, 888/226-7711, www.mohegansun.com • Foxwoods Resort Casino, 350 Trolley Line Blvd., Ledyard, CT, 860/312-3000, www.foxwoods.com • Encore Boston Harbor 1 Broadway, Everett, 857/770-7000, www.encorebostonharbor.com

Timing: The casino resorts are open year-round and offer a wide variety of activities, some of which (like hiking, golfing, and swimming) are better enjoyed in warmer months.

New Englanders love to gamble, and they don't have to go too far from their own backyards to try their luck at a poker table or slot machine. But New England's three largest casino resorts

▲ Mohegan Sun

aren't typical regional gambling halls: These are sprawling, multibillion-dollar Vegas-style resorts.

For years, Connecticut casino resorts **Mohegan Sun** and **Foxwoods Resort Casino** were the hubs of gaming activity in the northeastern U.S. Located on respective Native American reservations, Foxwoods and Mohegan Sun have massive gaming floors, a litany of fine dining options, and a wide range of activities for those who have zero interest in gambling. Both properties are about halfway between Boston and New York City and remain the most popular with loyal, local gamblers. Bus lines like Greyhound offer direct service to both properties from South Station in Boston.

Located about 1.5 hours southwest of Boston and operated by the Mohegan Tribe, **Mohegan Sun** looks like a standard glass hotel tower from the outside, but the resort has brightly-colored Native American-inspired design within. Waterfalls, fountains, a planetarium dome, and glass sculptures throughout the casino floor provide artistic contrast to the whirring and ringing bells of the slot machines. You can bring the whole family to Mohegan: the resort's arena attracts major acts like Jennifer Lopez and hosts sporting events, while the **Kids Quest arcade** keeps children under the age of 13 busy with games and activities. When you're hungry, **Frank Pepe Pizzeria Napoletana**—serving New Haven-style coal-fired pizza—can't be beat, but it's just one of 46 dining options to choose from. If you need to relax, you can unwind in the **Mandara Spa** or hit the fairway for a round of **golf** (note: the golf course has a dress code, www.mohegansun.com/mohegan-sun-golf-club.html).

Foxwoods, operated by the Mashantucket Pequot Tribal Nation, is a massive resort that includes two hotel towers and a six-casino complex just 1.5 hours southwest of Boston. Foxwoods opened in 1986 as a bingo hall before later adding games like poker and blackjack in the early 1990s. As the longest-running of the three major New England casinos, Foxwoods has a strong following and typically attracts an older crowd, but it also has family-friendly activities

▲ Foxwoods Resort Casino

like a zipline, arcade, and a museum about the Mashantucket Pequot Tribal Nation, so kids will enjoy a visit, too. The resort also has opportunities for atypical casino activities, like the

⌃ Encore Boston Harbor

marked **hiking trails** off the Grand Cedar Lobby, leading into the beautiful nearby Connecticut landscape, and **Ready Glaze Fire,** a paint-your-own pottery workshop. The exterior of the resort has a cool-toned blue and glass modern look. The interior has a warm, nature-inspired aesthetic, with lovely Native American-themed touches throughout. The resort's dining options range from familiar spots for quick bites (i.e. Starbucks and Auntie Anne's) to fancier lounges and fine dining restaurants. Check out **Cedars Steaks & Oysters,** a well-loved steakhouse with a raw bar and a good drink menu.

For Bostonians looking to gamble closer to home, there's **Encore Boston Harbor.** Encore is the largest casino in Massachusetts and arguably one of the most luxurious, sprawling resorts in the region. The curved, bronze tower is a notable addition to the Boston skyline and the shores of Boston Harbor. The resort grounds include lush gardens along the Mystic River with 20-foot stainless steel busts by artist Jaume Plensa. Inside, you'll find a flower-covered carousel in the lobby and the most iconic artwork in the casino's collection: a $28 million statue of Popeye by artist Jeff Koons. In the two-story gambling hall, you'll see everything from penny slots to by-invitation-only poker salons. The massive, column-filled space is covered in rich red and purple-hued carpeting while crimson lantern chandeliers dangle over banks of slot machines and poker tables. Encore is a glitzier resort, so nicer attire is recommended in lieu of athletic wear. Beyond gambling, waterfront gardens and a mix of craft beer bars and fancy Asian fusion restaurants and steakhouses are some of Encore's most popular attractions. **Rare Steakhouse** serves extremely high-end cuts of meat, including a $230, 4-ounce cut of Kobe beef (maybe save this one for when you hit the jackpot). **Night Shift Brewing Kitchen & Tap** is a more affordable option and serves up bar bites like chicken wings alongside Night Shift beers, brewed down the street in Everett. While Encore isn't a family-friendly place, non-gamblers still have plenty to do. The spa offers a wide range of treatments, including the Good Luck Ritual massage which is based on Chinese rituals to generate prosperity, happiness, and luck—everything one needs before hitting the casino floor! The casi-

History of Gambling in Boston

It hasn't been the easiest road to gambling in Greater Boston. State leaders considered legalizing it for years as a way to prevent losing so much money across state lines at properties like Mohegan Sun and Foxwoods. When casino gambling was finally legalized in 2011, it set off a wave of corporate competition for the most-prized license in Greater Boston (the state only allows one casino per designated region). Companies like Mohegan Sun, Wynn Resorts, and Caesars Entertainment battled it out for the Boston license.

Wynn Resorts won out, but then came under scrutiny close to opening day in 2019 in light of sexual misconduct allegations against its namesake founder, Steve Wynn. The company underwent a complete leadership overhaul, paid fines to the state of Massachusetts, and the resort—originally slated to be named Wynn Boston Harbor—got the new "Encore" name before the first slot machine even had a spin.

no offers a variety of transportation services, but the most fun may be the water taxi that runs from the Seaport and Long Wharf cruise terminals and drops you off right at Encore's front steps along the Mystic River.

The minimum **gambling age** at all resorts is **21.** All three casinos offer free drinks to gamblers on the casino floor, but service is often slow (be sure to tip servers a couple dollars with each drink). Photos aren't allowed on the casino floor, and don't try to sneak them anyway. Security cameras are everywhere! If you're planning a weekend trip, room rates can get expensive at each of the resorts, so opting for a nearby hotel can save you several hundred dollars each night.

Connect With...

28 Go to a concert

36 Go beyond Harvard Yard in Cambridge and Somerville

35 Get transcendental at Walden Pond

Get Outside • Architecture and Historic Spots • Day Trips

Why Go: Visiting Walden Pond is a perfect way to experience the great outdoors (and literary history) within minutes of some of the most congested streets of Boston and Cambridge.

Where: The Walden Pond State Reservation is about a half-hour northwest of Boston and Cambridge, accessible via Route 2 from Cambridge and via Interstates 90 and 95 from Boston. The Massachusetts State Parks service offers the most up-to-date information on trails, parking, and hours of operation. • https://www.mass.gov/locations/walden-pond-state-reservation

Timing: The park is open year-round for walks, running, and hiking, but summer is the best time to visit if you want to swim or boat in the pond. If you do head up in the summer, be sure to arrive early—parking lots fill up quickly! Boat ramps are closed from early December through early April.

Roughly half an hour from Harvard Square is Walden Pond State Reservation, just outside the town of Concord. Made famous by the transcendentalist Henry David Thoreau who wrote *Walden; or, Life in the Woods* here in the 1850s, beautiful Walden Pond has become a favorite destination for Bostonians looking to de-stress and unwind while enjoying the simple beauty of nature.

Far enough from the hustle and bustle of downtown Boston, the soundtrack of Walden Pond is filled with buzzing bees, chirping birds, splashing swimmers, and only the occasional sound of a passing commuter rail train on the western shore. With sandy beaches along the pond and miles of tree-lined, winding trails, the reservation is the perfect place to visit if you're looking for a little outdoor adventure. Birds, squirrels, and rabbits are among the most common forms of wildlife in the area; however, foxes, skunks, and raccoons are also known to wander out in the morning and at night.

In warmer months, the 102-foot deep pond is great for swimming, boating, and fishing. Though simply lounging on the sand with a good book is lovely, too. Swimming and kayaking

▲ the shore of Walden Pond

▲ Walden Pond

▲ canoeing on the pond

(bring your own, as rentals are not provided) are some of the popular activities to do with kids. A Walden Pond beach day is more relaxing than those at some of the more raucous beaches of South Boston; pets, grilling, and blow-up water toys are all prohibited here. You might say the state park service is just trying to keep things in the transcendental spirit of Thoreau!

If a beach day doesn't seem appealing, you can take advantage of the hiking and walking paths. I like to jog along the nearly two-mile Pond Path—especially on a crisp morning when the reservation is less crowded—but the more secluded trails on the west side of the pond are fun, too. Emerson's Cliff Trail and Heywood's Meadow Path are also notable, but Pond Path is the best way to get a comprehensive overview of most of the popular areas of the park. This generally flat, 1.7-mile loop around Walden Pond passes by the plaque marking the site of Thoreau's original cabin, as well as swimming beaches, boat launches, and forests. Stop by the visitors center for a free trail map.

Those interested in learning more about Thoreau's time here can also check out the repli-

▲ statue of Henry David Thoreau by artist Jo Davidson

Thoreau at Walden Pond

A city that prides itself on its history and culture as Boston does obviously cherishes a place like Walden Pond, which not only contributes to the region's extensive network of parks but also inspired one of the most revered pieces of American literature.

Henry David Thoreau spent two years in his cabin in the woods pondering the human condition, or, as he put it: "I wished to live deliberately." Thoreau had significantly more solitude during his reflective time at Walden Pond, but visitors today can still benefit from this largely intact nature preserve.

ca of his single-room cabin. Channel your inner Transcendentalist by keeping a journal handy to jot down whatever thoughts the landscape might inspire.

Pack your own snacks for the day and take advantage of the scenic picnic areas. You'll also want to bring money for parking ($8 for MA residents, $30 for non-residents).

Note: The reservation has restrooms, so there's really no excuse for relieving yourself in the water. Years of such activity contaminated the pond, and it was closed for recreational swimming. Preservationists have since fixed that problem (and swimming is once again safe), so let's keep it that way.

Connect With...

36 Go beyond Harvard Yard in Cambridge and Somerville

43 Head East on the Mohawk Trail

36 Go beyond Harvard Yard
in Cambridge and Somerville

Day Trips • Architecture and Historic Spots

Why Go: Harvard and MIT are the two visitor magnets for Cambridge, a city separated from Boston by the Charles River. But these storied learning institutions have fueled a building boom in Cambridge and the neighboring city of Somerville, which have become lovely towns with exciting restaurant scenes and plenty of charm.

Where: The easiest way to get to Cambridge and Somerville is on the MBTA's Red Line subway. Most Cambridge destinations are within walking distance of three stops (Kendall, Central Square, and Harvard), while Somerville's best hotspots are found near the Davis MBTA station.

Timing: Autumn strolls around Cambridge and Somerville are the most scenic, with the changing leaves and the spectacle of the Head of the Charles Regatta. But winter is a good time to curl up in a cozy Harvard Square restaurant or Davis Square speakeasy. Spring can be rather hectic, especially during graduation season. Visit in summer to get sunny days without as many students.

The green, lush lawn and Georgian and Federal style architecture of Harvard Yard pulls visitors from around the world jockeying for a place at the prestigious Ivy League university. Some even

▲ Harvard Square

rub the left foot of a statue of John Harvard on the gated lawn for good luck ahead of the exhaustive application process, hoping to make it into an incoming freshman class. But for those of us who rubbed the foot and still got rejected, I highly recommend skipping the campus and enjoying Harvard's surrounding neighborhoods for collegiate vibes and beautiful architecture without all the stress of mid-terms and finals.

Harvard Square and nearby Davis Square in Somerville (two stops north on the MBTA Red Line subway) have always been popular with college students, but they are also becoming more popular with the post-grad crowd. The growing food scene, fun nightlife, and an array of interesting shopping options surrounded by historic buildings all lend to the youthful energy here.

The bustling, red-brick neighborhood of Harvard Square sits between the Charles River and Harvard University. Though small in size, Harvard Square is full to the brim with retail stores and eateries. It's also home to some of Harvard's clubs and organizations, including the school's prestigious newspaper, *The Harvard Crimson*. Start your exploration of the neighborhood in the plaza at the intersection of Massachusetts Avenue, Brattle Street, and John F. Kennedy Street. You can pick up a map of the area from the Cambridge Visitor Information Booth.

To the west of the information booth, between Brattle and Church Streets, is the usually crowded **Atrium shopping center** (50 Church St.), which has a great mix of popular retail chains and local shops. **Milk Bar** (3 Brattle St., 857/321-8430, www.milkbarstore.com) is a New York City-based dessert shop that has found loyal fans in Beantown; **Cardullo's Gourmet Shoppe** (6 Brattle St., 617/491-8888, www.cardullos.com) has everything from sweet treats, grocery items, and spirits to stock your liquor cabinet; and the women-owned **Mint Julep** (43 Brattle St., 617/576-6468, www.shopmintjulep.com) clothing boutique nearby is a popular local shop for unique fashion finds. The Atrium is also home to the **Harvard Coop** (1400 Massachusetts Ave., 617/499-2000, www.store.thecoop.com), a massive bookstore shared by Harvard and MIT.

Southeast of the shopping plaza, you can follow Mt. Auburn Street to the neighborhood's southeast edge, admiring the architecture along the way. Stop by the **Harvard Lampoon** (44 Bow St.), a copper-domed brick structure adorned with an ibis on top (the bird logo of the famous student humor magazine). Next door is a narrow Flemish architecture building with an imposing brick façade that has led some to refer to it as the Lampoon Castle.

Continue along Mt. Auburn Street until you reach Plympton Street. Turn left on Plympton to take a stroll past some of Harvard's dormitories, including Randolph Hall and Apthorp House on the west side of the street and Westmorely Hall on the east. This stretch of residence halls between Bow Street and Massachusetts Avenue was once referred to as the "Gold Coast." The dorms were built at the turn of the century for some of Harvard's wealthiest undergraduates. When you're done admiring the buildings, pop into the nearby indie **Harvard Book Store** (1256 Massachusetts Ave., 617/661-1515); it's a great spot to find a bestseller on the main retail floor or a quirky used book down in the basement.

For those more interested in dining than shopping, the restaurant scene in Harvard Square has become impressively varied, with tons of options for a tasty meal. Grab a bite to eat at one of the popular hangouts like **Alden & Harlow** (40 Brattle St., 617/864-2100, www.aldenharlow. com), which serves inventive New American dishes, or **Waypoint** (1030 Massachusetts Ave., 617/864-2300, www.waypointharvard.com), which will satisfy any fishy cravings. Decades-old **Grendel's Den Restaurant & Bar** (89 Winthrop St., 617/491-1160, www.grendelsden.com) is a great option for those wishing to enjoy pub food with a side of college gossip.

If you're visiting the area in October, join crew enthusiasts from all over who come to Harvard Square and the banks of the Charles River to see the annual **Head of the Charles Regatta** (www.hocr.org), the largest 2-day regatta in the world.

Further up the T's Red Line from Harvard Square is Somerville's more-compact Davis Square. Though you may not run into many MIT or Harvard students here, you will encounter students from nearby Tufts University, so you'll still get the energetic, collegiate vibe of Harvard Square while enjoying this less crowded area. From the T station, you can take College Avenue to Elm Street and head down Elm in either direction to explore the area. Davis Square has more of a mix of young professionals, graduate students, and undergraduates mingling along its streets of bars and restaurants.

While exploring, stop by the **Somerville Theatre** (55 Davis Square, 617/625-5700, www. somervilletheatre.com), a movie theatre/concert hall and home of the **Museum of Bad Art** (781/444-6757, www.museumofbadart.org). An ode to all things never to be found in the Louvre, the MOBA is located near the theatre's restrooms and showcases about 25 pieces at a time from its more than 700-piece collection. Bad is in the eye of the beholder at this museum of art gone awry, but you can get an idea of what's in store based on this description of *Pauline Resting*, a painting of a nude woman rescued from a Boston trashcan: "MOBA curators believe this painting, as well as others in the collection, may have been affected by the artists' never having actually seen a naked woman."

Davis Square is undergoing a bit of a transformation, trying to retain some of the old while ushering in plenty of new; that's especially obvious in the restaurant scene. Longtime residents can still grab **Flatbread Company**'s (45 Day St., 617/776-0552, www.flatbreadcompany.com) organic wood-fired pizza and play candlepin bowling at **Sacco's Bowl Haven.** But there are

Ivy League Rivalries: MIT and Harvard

The top Ivy League rivalry may belong to Harvard and Yale, but the Crimson have another (friendlier) foe just two subway stops away. Harvard and MIT draw natural comparisons due to their respective internationally renowned curriculum and academic prowess. MIT is traditionally the more scientific-minded university, while Harvard is steeped in its history of churning out political and business leaders since the founding of our country.

MIT's Great Dome makes it the most noticeable campus from downtown Boston, but Harvard Yard is the more picturesque of the two. The biggest reason Harvard likely views MIT as a threat is due to MIT's great success in turning the once overlooked Kendall Square neighborhood into the world's leading hub of life science innovation. Pharmaceutical and tech companies have poured into Kendall to tap into the potential workforce being educated nearby. Cranes dot the skyline due to so many companies coveting a piece of real estate here.

Harvard, in turn, has turned its attention to expanding its Allston campus into its own version of a tech hub—to the point that Harvard actually now has more property in Boston than its hometown of Cambridge.

plenty of other places to explore: cuisines range from Thai to Mexican to southern barbeque at the ever-expanding list of restaurants up and down Holland and Elm Streets and Highland Avenue.

There's no better example of this area's ability to embrace change while still honoring the old than **Rosebud American Kitchen & Bar** (381 Summer St., 617/629-9500, www.rosebudkitchen.com), which was formerly a diner. Still very much in its classic digs, the new iteration of the Rosebud is more about red leather booths and sultry cocktails than hangover food on a Sunday morning.

Harvard Yard may be the most popular spot to visit in the Cambridge area, but Harvard Square and nearby Davis Square are just as worthy of your time.

Connect With...

18 Cheer on runners at the Boston Marathon
20 Kayak the Charles River
34 Try your luck at New England casinos

37 Celebrate Pride

in Provincetown

Boston Parties • Weekend Getaways

Why Go: Discover why this small town on the Outer Cape embraced the LGBTQ+ community, which embraced it right back. Pride here goes well beyond the month of June: It's a year-round celebration.

Where: The outer tip of Cape Cod at the end of Route 6 takes about 2.5 hours (factoring in a quick rest stop) if driving from Boston. Many find it easier (though more expensive) to fly via Cape Air from Boston's Logan International Airport or take a fast ferry from Boston's Seaport or Long Wharf. • www.provincetown-ma.gov, www.cityexperiences.com/boston, www.baystatecruisecompany.com, www.capeair.com

Timing: Given the number of beaches, restaurants, shops, and drag shows to check out in Ptown, I recommend a weekend trip. Between Memorial Day and Labor is peak Ptown, with all seasonal venues open and larger crowds and higher prices on hotel rooms. The spring and fall shoulder seasons are more affordable and less crowded, but there aren't as many drag shows, and some restaurants and stores aren't open.

Whether arriving by land, sea, or air, there is nothing quite as exciting as that first glimpse of Provincetown's Pilgrim Monument. The unofficial welcome mat to Ptown, a granite tower noting the Pilgrims arrived here before scooting across Cape Cod Bay to Plymouth, lords over the tip of the Cape as one of many signs this isn't like any of its neighboring beachy towns.

The small cluster of fishing boats perennially located in Provincetown Harbor occasionally blare out a foghorn, indicating the town hasn't totally lost sight of its fishing and whaling roots. But the blast of rainbow flags, parades down **Commercial Street** (the town's main thoroughfare), and bass beats from an array of nightclubs in the summer are all proof that the Ptown of today is much more of a haven for a good time than a seafood collection. Still, no matter why you visit, this town accepts all with open arms and open minds.

What might surprise you is that Ptown only had its first Pride weekend in 2018, but the town celebrates LGBTQ+ Pride all year long. Themed weekends range from **Snowbound Leather** in February for the leather community, the **Memorial Day Weekend Lesbian Festival**, and July's **Bear Week** for members of this more burly segment of the community

▲ sunset in Provincetown

▲ rainbow-colored frozen rosé

▲ Pride flag in the Provincetown Marina

▲ Carnival Parade

(for those of us who still can't grow a beard, Bear allies are welcome, too!). The designated **Pride Weekend** itself is more of a low-key event in early June with the most visible element being a 20-mile long laser display of the rainbow colors of the LGBTQ+ flag running across Provincetown Harbor.

As you get further into the dog days of summer, August's **Carnival Week** is a Ptown holiday with an annual theme giving residents and visitors an excuse to dress up and parade down Commercial St. The 1980s theme of the 2016 event led to a mob of drag Madonnas (present company included) filling the streets and striking poses. And powder blue gingham was hard to come by when everyone planned out their Dorothy costume for 2021's "Somewhere Over the Rainbow" theme.

Theme weeks run Saturday to Saturday (and most vacation rentals on platforms like Airbnb will only allow you to book a stay by the week for this reason). While the weekend themes may vary, visitors still utilize or frequent many of the same venues to make the most of their trip.

In addition to the year-round Pride events, Provincetown has great restaurants and shops. **Pepe's Wharf Restaurant** (371 Commercial St., 508/487-8717, www.pepeswharf.com), the **Red Inn** (15 Commercial St., 508/487-7334, www.theredinn.com), and **Jimmy's HideAway** (179 Commercial St., 508/487-1011, www.jimmyshideaway.com) have cozy, seaside dining rooms serving up fresh seafood and steaks.

Shops owned and operated by members and allies of the LGBTQ+ community like **Perry's Fine Wines and Liquors** (1 Tremont St., 508/487-0140, www.ptownperrys.com), **Pop+Dutch** (147 Commercial St., 774/538-6472, www.popanddutch.com), and **Relish Bakery & Sandwich Shop** (93 Commercial St., 508/487-8077, www.ptownrelish.com) offer all the necessary ingredients you never knew you needed for a decadent picnic on the beach. Perry's co-owners Charlie Greener and Billy Marshall's encyclopedic knowledge of fine food and wines will up the ante on your happy hour with Sancerre, rosé, specialty foods, and a case of various vintages to take home. Relish is a great spot for grab & go breakfast sandwiches or baked goods like tarts or scones.

Pop+Dutch has a cult following due to their menu of mouth-watering breakfast sandwiches (always upgrade to a biscuit for your bread of choice) in the morning and salads and sandwiches in the afternoon—always enhanced with a side of chips and pimento cheese (as

Commercial Street

delicious as any I've had in the South, and I've had a lot of pimento cheese!). Keep an eye out for co-owners Sean Gardner and Rebecca Orchant's wide variety of daily specials, which range from Cajun red beans and rice to strawberry rhubarb pies.

It should be obvious by now that there's no shortage of fun to be had in Ptown. Summer afternoons are ruled by afternoon tea (dance parties with booze) at the **Boatslip Resort & Beach Club** (161 Commercial St., 508/487-1669, www.theboatslip.com). When same-sex couples weren't allowed to dance together, the gay community called their dances "afternoon tea" to disguise the events, an idea that caught on and spread across the country. In Ptown, tea at the Boatslip goes from 4pm until 7pm on the waterfront. Be sure to try at least one Planter's Punch, a deceptively potent rum concoction that will have you twirling on the dance floor in no time.

For the night owls, places like the **A-House** (6 Masonic Place #4, 508/487-3169, www.ahouse.com) and **Paramount Bar** at the **Crown & Anchor** (247 Commercial St., 408/487-1430, www.onlyatthecrown.com) are popular dance floors that stay busy right up until last call at 1am.

The A House is not only one of the oldest gay bars in the U.S., it's one of the oldest-running bars period—parts of the building date all the way back to 1798. The colonial vibes, occasional fireplaces, creaky wooden floors, and booming DJ stand make the A House unlike most LGBTQ+ dance floors, while Paramount is a more modern disco hub with light shows and dancers on platforms. Paramount and the surrounding Crown & Anchor resort complex are typically hubs for activity during themed weeks of the year, offering everything from drag shows to the nightclub experience.

The best way to get around Ptown is by bike. **Rent a bike** from one of the local shops; **Arnold's Bike Shop** (329 Commercial St., 508/487-0844, www.provincetownbikes.com) and **Provincetown Bike Rentals** (136 Bradford St., 774/447-4539, www.provincetownbikerentals.com) are the most centrally located. Sunscreen is a must for lounging at Race Point and Herring Cove beaches, but a light sweater is good for windy days — it's not unheard of for Ptown to be 20 degrees cooler than Boston on a spring or summer day.

Summer is by far the busiest time to visit Ptown and also the season with the most ac-

▲ Provincetown Bike Rentals

Inspiring and Welcoming Ptown

The local joke is the Pilgrims stopped in Provincetown Harbor, dropped off the drag queens, and then continued to Plymouth Rock. While I'm not aware of a colonial-era Bianca del Rio, plenty of major names have passed through and been inspired by these sandy shores. Given its remote location at the tip of Cape Cod, Ptown has always held a reputation as a refuge for a variety of people, especially the LGBTQ+ community when the rest of the country wasn't as accepting as it is today.

Author and summer resident Michael Cunningham described it succinctly in his travelogue and highly observational *Land's End: A Walk in Provincetown*: "It is the Morocco of America, the New Orleans of the north." Tennessee Williams was so inspired during his four summers in Ptown that he reportedly worked on several of his iconic plays like *A Streetcar Named Desire* and *The Glass Menagerie* while in residence.

tivities and themed weeks; however, the shoulder seasons—spring and fall—are great times to enjoy Ptown with thousands less people jamming the streets and a greater likelihood of a deal on Airbnb. Halloween and Christmas are also popular themed weeks with nightclubs open and visitors encouraged to dress up. The timing of the themed weeks varies each year, so head to www.ptowntourism.com for the latest information.

The drive from Boston is typically 2.5 hours, but it can get significantly longer in summer months due to Cape Cod traffic. The easier (but costlier) way to get to Provincetown is via the 90-minute fast ferries that leave from the World Trade Center terminal in Boston's Seaport neighborhood or from Long Wharf. The fastest (and costliest) option is a 20-minute Cape Air flight from Boston Logan International Airport.

Connect With...

41 Slurp oysters in Wellfleet

42 Cruise Cape Cod on Old King's Highway

44 Get your feet wet at New England's best beaches

38 Get inspired at Mass MoCA

Art and Culture • Day Trips

Why Go: The Massachusetts Museum of Contemporary Art is a great, cultural motivation to head to western Massachusetts for a day or, even better, a weekend to explore the surrounding Berkshires region.

Where: Mass MoCA is a little over two-and-a-half hours northwest of Boston on Route 2. The easiest way to get there is to drive. • 1040 Mass MoCA Way, North Adams, 413/662-2111, www.massmoca.org

Timing: Fall is my favorite time to visit the museum, as it is also a perfect time to take in the colorful foliage in the Berkshires. But there is plenty to do year-round and particularly in non-winter months: Mass MoCA offers live events with dance and musical performances 40 weekends out of the year. You can spend at least an entire afternoon at the museum but incorporating it into a weekend trip is even better.

You may not expect one of the biggest forces of contemporary art in New England to be well beyond the confines of Boston's urban core, but the Massachusetts Museum of Contemporary Art, also known as Mass MoCA, is just that: 26 restored, red-brick factory buildings in the Berkshires enclave of North Adams, packed with modern art.

Spencer Finch, *Cosmic Latte*

Part of the Mass MoCA experience is the drive into Western Massachusetts and the Berkshires. The green forests and mountains make you feel like you're a million miles away from Boston. I remember the first time I visited Mass MoCA and that feeling of being transported to an old mill town as we pulled up. The museum feels approachable, without the intimidating stonework or ultra-modern exteriors of other museums. The campus is less like a palace for art and more of a welcoming meeting place for all kinds of art lovers.

While I love Boston's contemporary art venues like the Museum of Fine Art and the Institute of Contemporary Art, nothing offers the same variety of mediums as Mass MoCA. Enor-

entrance to Mass MoCA

Natalie Jeremijenko, *Tree Logic*

Sol LeWitt, *Wall Drawing 692*

mous galleries as well as indoor and outdoor performing arts spaces accommodate showcases on canvas, sculpture, stage, sound, and beyond. The museum is unique in that it is meant to house more of a "living" collection rather than a permanent one; therefore, you'll see more long-term exhibitions that can last decades rather than something that stays with the museum forever.

One of the most popular (and easily recognizable to the ear) pieces at the museum is **Christina Kubisch's *Clocktower Project***, which involved restoring a more than 100-year-old clocktower outside the museum and outfitting it with solar sensors to chime on the hour with different sounds depending on how sunny it is outside. A nice day outside will spark loud, cheery bells while a cloudy day will sound more somber.

In 2005, the museum was home to former artist-in-residence **David Cole**'s ***The Knitting Machine***. The massive sculptural installation was made up of two John Deere excavators equipped with 20-foot knitting needles and yarn in order to knit an American flag. When the flag was complete, it was folded into a triangle just shy of the size of a Volkswagen Beetle and placed in a case beside a video of the excavators completing the flag.

In 2018, the museum's Hunter Hallway gallery space showcased a massive cut-paper collage work by **Natasha Bowdoin,** called ***Maneater***. Multicolor floral forms, including carnivorous and thorny plants, covered the walls and some of the floor, devouring the viewer in the space.

Mass MoCA also attracts artists you wouldn't think necessarily belong in a museum. Singer-songwriter **Annie Lennox's 2019 art installation** made up of her personal objects served as a career retrospective, showcasing her strong history of activism.

One of the more psychological exhibits in 2011, appropriately titled ***Memery: Imitation, Memory, and Internet Culture***, used memes and various Internet platforms (YouTube, Tumblr, social networking sites, etc.) to explore whether the world wide web was the source of entirely useless bits of pop culture or if there was something deeper to these viral moments. Unfortunately, that exhibit came a few years before TikTok, or I'm sure it wouldn't have bothered with the whole "deeper meaning" part (I kid!).

These are just a few samples of the wide variety of artistic accomplishments on display at the giant Mass MoCA campus. Check the website before visiting to see current exhibits—or

Origins: Mass MoCA

The 26 buildings that comprise the museum are on a site with industrial roots dating back before the Revolutionary War. Shoes, cabinets, hats, fabrics, and even components of the atomic bomb have all been manufactured on the Mass MoCA property at some point during its history. Today, it's all about artistic masterpieces, but the property still has the look of an industrial mill rather than one of the world's leading contemporary art museums.

The last industrial tenant of the Mass MoCA property was the Sprague Electric Company, whose employees were contracted by the U.S. government during World War II to produce electrical parts for weapons systems like the atomic bomb. The Sprague factory eventually shuttered in 1985, and leaders in North Adams immediately got to work pursuing ways to renovate the property for alternative uses. The team at the art museum of nearby Williams College voiced interest in finding space to exhibit works of art, and the seeds of a contemporary art museum were planted. But it wasn't until 1999, after years of fundraising, that Mass MoCA finally opened its doors.

just let yourself be surprised. Whether you visit with an agenda or want to simply wander, it's easy to spend an entire day at this Berkshires gem. Be sure to give yourself enough time to explore the Mass MoCA store, a must-stop for souvenirs and affordable print versions of what you'll see in the galleries.

When you get hungry, head to the tasty spots onsite. **A-oK Berkshire Barbecue** serves up mouth-watering smoked chicken and pulled pork sandwiches (there are vegan options, too!). **Lickety Split** offers local ice cream and café fare. Stop by **Bright Ideas Brewing** for refreshing beer, which might just be as much of a draw as the museum itself. For those making the drive back to Boston in the same day, an espresso from **Tunnel City Coffee** is the smarter after-museum beverage.

Connect With...

43 Head East on the Mohawk Trail
51 Rejuvenate in the Berkshires

39 Find quintessential New England in Newburyport

Day Trips

Why Go: For the varied group torn between a beach getaway or finding a cute town in which to shop and dine, Newburyport has a little bit of everything for everyone.

Where: Newburyport is a 45-minute drive north of Boston near the New Hampshire border on the Atlantic Ocean coast. It can also be reached in just over an hour on the commuter rail from Boston's North Station.

Timing: Newburyport and Plum Island can be enjoyed year-round.

There are oodles of cute seaside towns up and down the coast of New England—yet I find myself returning, at least once a year, to Newburyport and adjoining Plum Island. The mix of boutique shopping, cobblestoned streets, delectable restaurants, and seaside views in just a few blocks packs a lot into this coastal enclave. Nearby Plum Island is a barrier island and home to some of the more popular beaches where Newburyport locals go in the warmer months. The sandy dunes and expansive coastline make this a great spot for beach picnicking, sunbathing, and playing in the waves.

I'm the weirdo who loves a beach trip in the winter, and I was lucky enough to have a dear friend introduce me to **Blue - Inn on the Beach** (20 Fordham Way, 978/463-6128, www.blueinn.com). The inn quickly became my favorite home base for every trip to Newburyport; the rooms are cozy (most have fireplaces for winter treks) with stunning views of the Atlantic Ocean, and a daily breakfast basket is included with your stay. The inn is directly on the beach and also a quick drive (or leisurely stroll) from amazing on-island dining options. **Plum Island Grille** (2 Plum Island Turnpike, #2035, 978/463-2290, www.plumislandgrille.com) offers scrumptious seafood in a cozy dining room, and **Mad Martha's Café** (51 Northern Blvd., 978/462-7707, www.madmarthaislandcafe.com) is a funky beach shack offering an all-American breakfast spread.

For those shying away from the beach in cooler months, shopping and dining in down-

boardwalk trail on Plum Island

town Newburyport is a great way to spend an afternoon and evening. Just a 10-minute drive west from Plum Island, downtown Newburyport is stocked with historic brick buildings housing a bevy of boutique shopping and restaurants.

It's hard *not* to shop local in Newburyport, as there are so many mom-and-pop shops in such a small area. The **Tannery Marketplace** (50 Water St., 978/465-7047, www.tannerymarketplace.com) is a former mill that has been renovated into a retail mecca, with home stores and specialty food shops. **Jabberwocky Bookshop** (www.jabberwockybookshop.com) in the marketplace is a very popular spot for browsing and readings, and women-led **Joppa Fine Foods** (www.joppafinefoods.com) is the go-to store to stock up on decadent snack and meal options if you're considering a picnic on the beach later.

Best of British (22 State St., 978/465-6976, www.bestofbritishnbpt.com), in the heart of downtown, is a fun spot to drop in for, as the name suggests, all sorts of clothes, accessories, and food items from the UK. **The Coffee Factory** (56 State St., 978/358-7539, www.mycoffeefactory.net) is where to fuel up with a latte or frozen coffee to start the day or recharge before a night on the town.

Newburyport also has a decent cluster of breweries for beer lovers just to the southwest of downtown.

Newburyport Brewing Co. (4 New Pasture Rd., 978/463-8700, www.nbptbrewing.com) has a marquee line-up of New England- and West Coast-style IPAs, as well as the local-inspired Newburyport Pale Ale and Plum Island Belgian White. **RiverWalk Brewing Co.** (40 Parker St., 978/499-2337, www.riverwalkbrewing.com) has a taproom of 12 rotating drafts as well as a menu stocked with hearty bar food like empanadas and grilled sausages. Rounding out the brewery trio is **House Bear Brewing** (3 Graf Rd., #15, 978/388-1506, www.housebearbrewing.com), an award-winning mead-focused brewery, with tasty options like passion fruit and strawberry basil meads.

Whether you're in town to stroll along the quaint streets, shop for local gems, taste-test craft brews, or enjoy a pensive stroll along the gorgeous coastline, Newburyport can feel like a world away from the hustle of Boston despite its convenient location less than an hour away. Take advantage of the convenience and set aside a day to make the quick trip north.

Origins: Newburyport

Newburyport's historic industries were shipbuilding and liquor distilling (the city, unfortunately, played an important role in the triangle trade of slavery, sugar, and rum). Those industries, like in many other parts of New England, died out. But while cities farther inland still grapple with hulking, abandoned mills, Newburyport has managed to transform itself into a highly popular summer tourist destination, due in part to its revitalized mills and downtown area that now focus heavily on retail, dining, and bars.

Connect With...

46 Taste foodie paradise in Portland, Maine
49 Shop local in Portsmouth, New Hampshire

40 Go apple-picking

Get Outside • Day Trips • Fun for Families and Kids

Why Go: A fall apple-picking trek is a treasured New England pastime.

Where: Carver Hill Orchard, 101 Brookside Ave., Stow, 978/897-6177, www.carverhill-orchard.com • Smolak Farms, 315 S Bradford St., North Andover, 978/682-6332, www.smolakfarms.com • Dowse Farms, 30 Rockwood St., Sherborn, 508/653-2639, www.dowseorchards.com

Timing: September and October are the best times to visit the orchards, but some, like Carver Hill Orchard, begin their picking season as early as July.

In the "basic" hierarchy, it probably doesn't get more basic than a fall trek in plaid shirts and chinos to an orchard for apple-picking and apple cider donuts. But tradition is tradition, and there is something magical and festive about wandering around a Massachusetts farm with close friends, breathing in the crisp fall air.

Apple-picking season is one of my favorite times to get just beyond the city and collect ingredients for some impressive farm-to-table pies. Lucky for me (and for you), there are several farms less than an hour outside Boston to satisfy fruit and cider cravings. No matter the farm, you'll need to purchase their empty bags and containers, varying in size (typically $10-30), before venturing out into the orchards and farms for fresh produce. Fruit and veggie ripeness and availability are dependent on weather from year to year, so each year can bring an unexpected surprise, like late-season fruit, or an unpleasant disappointment, like fewer fruity options than you hoped. It's never a bad idea to call ahead to see what's in season and ready for picking!

Carver Hill Orchard, 40 minutes northwest of Boston in Stow, Massachusetts, is a favorite among farm-to-table home cooks due to the variety of pick-your-own produce on-site. Depending on when you visit, you can pick blueberries, tomatoes, peppers, beans, peaches, and zucchini, in addition to varieties of Snow White's fruity nemesis, thanks to the farm's extended season, which runs from July through November. Carver Hill also has a great country store,

▲ apple tree

▲ apple cider donuts

▲ picked apples

where visitors can buy cider, cheese, local meats and eggs, as well as jams and honey. Don't skip the warm cider donuts!

Smolak Farms, about 40 minutes north of the city in Andover, Massachusetts, is a family-friendly apple-picking experience, complete with hayrides, farm animals, and a kids' playground. Smolak offers fruit-picking tours to educate guests on the right time to pick apples, blueberries, strawberries, and pumpkins, setting it apart from other farms in the area. Their weekly farm stand provides delicious to-go meals, including pizzas, potpies, and quiches—but, really, do you need a full meal when you can go straight to the apple pie and cider donuts?

Two hundred years old and still kicking, **Dowse Farms,** 40 minutes southwest of the city in Sherborn, Massachusetts, is among the oldest farms in the region. Along with 20 varieties of apples and a pumpkin patch, Dowse Farms also grows flowers, Christmas trees, and seasonal fruits and vegetables, offering fun for all seasons! Mums in the fall are a nice touch in the kitchen, so a Dowse Farms trip is more my speed when I'm trying to go that extra Martha Stewart mile. (As Queen Martha would say, "It's a good thing.")

A farm customer picks a pumpkin.

A Brief History of Apple-Picking in New England

According to the New England Apples industry group, the region's apple-growing (and picking) tradition started shortly after the first European immigrants arrived in the 1600s and noticed the lack of apples. Only a few kinds of crabapples were growing in the region. Records of apple seeding and harvesting date back to three years after the Pilgrims arrived in Plymouth in 1620. Roughly 30 different varieties of apples are commercially produced across New England today, with McIntosh apples as the biggest crop.

New England produces as much as 4 million 42-pound boxes of fresh apples each year, with Massachusetts being the largest producer.

No matter which farm you decide to visit, you'll probably see a trend in terms of clothing (think plaid shirts, Ray-Ban sunglasses, and Sperry Top-Siders duck boots), as well as many people taking selfies to pair with pun-y hashtags like #TheseAreTheApplesOfMyEye. Don't worry; you don't have to wear the unofficial New England fall uniform or share your experience on social media to have an excellent and memorable time on your apple-picking excursion (of course, you can if you want to). Do wear sturdy shoes and light layers, though; the boots and plaid aren't entirely for looks. In especially wet fall seasons, the farms and orchards can get pretty muddy.

Connect With...

35 Get transcendental at Walden Pond
43 Head East on the Mohawk Trail

41
Slurp oysters
in Wellfleet

Drink and Dine • Day Trips

Why Go: Nantucket, Martha's Vineyard, and areas "down Cape" tend to get the heaviest summer crowds, as visitors flock to their beaches. Even Provincetown, at the very end of Cape Cod, gets packed due to its relatively easy access via the Provincetown Fast Ferry. But Wellfleet is known for more than just beaches. Its eponymous oyster is a mainstay in seafood restaurants, so head straight to the source to slurp down a dozen (or more) of these briny delicacies.

Where: Bostonians reliably use the flexed arm as a Cape Cod map, and Wellfleet is about halfway up the forearm. It's about a two-hour drive from downtown Boston.

Timing: Wellfleet is a fairly easy day trip, especially if you're planning on timing your visit around OysterFest in October. Leave Boston by mid-morning to arrive just in time for lunch. The late afternoon drive home can be longer, especially in peak summer months when traffic on Route 6 backs up from everyone leaving the Cape.

The Wellfleet Oyster is an integral part of any New England restaurant menu, as these smooth bivalves are a popular meal starter. Often overlooked by crowds passing through en route to Provincetown to the north, the fishing town of Wellfleet is the mecca of the authentic New England oyster experience. From beach shacks to fine dining, the Wellfleet Oyster's namesake town offers many ways to enjoy a few of these salty gems of the sea.

Before we delve into where you can sample Wellfleet's oysters, let's talk basics: ordering and eating. Whether you're a novice or a raw bar regular, it's standard to start with a dozen oysters for the table. Add a dash of horseradish, red wine vinegar, or a squeeze of lemon (common seasoning staples that generally come with all orders) to each slippery delight to give them an extra kick, and then slurp them off the half shell and let them slide down your throat. (Some shells may need a little tap on your teeth to fully dislodge the oyster.) If possible, try to add oysters from other regions for a fun taste test comparison. For example, West Coast oysters are noticeably sweeter than the Wellfleet variety.

Now, let's discuss where to find these seaside treats. Wellfleet spans from the shores of

an oyster farm in Wellfleet

Wellfleet beach

oysters

Cape Cod Bay across to the Atlantic, so there are numerous seafood eateries to choose from. Experiences range from oysters shucked right in front of you to more glamorous presentations on ice in a formal dining room.

The best-known spot in Wellfleet is **The Beachcomber** (1120 Cahoon Hollow Rd., 508/349-6055, www.thebeachcomber.com), a rickety beach shack from the outside but boisterous bar, restaurant, and dance club on the inside. Located at the top of the dunes at Cahoon Hollow Beach on the Atlantic Ocean side of town, the Beachcomber (or 'Comber, as locals call it) loses about a row of parking each year due to beach erosion, so enjoy the oysters, dancing, and live music while you can! Typically open from Memorial Day to Labor Day, the 'Comber offers fried and grilled seafood at bar-style seating and picnic tables. Oysters are shucked outside from a raw bar overlooking the Atlantic and are best enjoyed on summer nights along with a Goombay Smash (rum punch). My favorite thing about the 'Comber: nobody gets cell phone reception inside.

If you don't know any fishfolk who can shuck oysters for you off the back of their boats,

▲ PB Boulangerie Bistro

Oyster Farming in Wellfleet Harbor

Colonists who settled in mainland areas like Plymouth flocked to Wellfleet Harbor's abundant fishing areas dating as far back as the 1600s. At the time, they referred to the area as Billingsgate, after a famed London fish market. It was eventually named Wellfleet after oysters found on the eastern coast of England. Overfishing and the later establishment of the Cape Cod National Seashore limited the town's booming industry. But oyster farming has taken off. It takes about two to three years for an oyster to go from seed on the aquatic farm to shucking in a restaurant. Roughly 850,000 oysters are reportedly harvested each year from Wellfleet waters.

Mac's Shack (91 Commercial St., 508/349-6333, www.macsseafood.com) and the **Pearl Restaurant & Bar** (250 Commercial St., 508/349-2999, www.wellfleetpearl.com) can fill that role. Located steps from where the boats come into Wellfleet Harbor, both Mac's and the Pearl are popular with locals craving a cocktail and some seafood. The Pearl even has live music for a serenade while you slurp. These two reliable local spots offer views of Wellfleet Harbor, where much of their raw bars originate. While neither have formal dining rooms, they are less raucous than the quasi-nightclub atmosphere of the Beachcomber.

For those wanting a more highbrow oyster experience, **PB Boulangerie Bistro** (15 Lecount Hollow Rd., 508/349-1600, www.pbboulangeriebistro.com) serves their oysters as a starter to fine French cuisine.

If you feel like getting festive with your oysters, the annual **Wellfleet OysterFest** (www.wellfleetspat.org) in October is a two-day celebration of the town's shellfish culture. Thousands of people turn up on the streets of Wellfleet to indulge in oysters, chowder (even chowder fries!), and other New England fare from an array of food vendors. The weekend is full of fun with the All Star Shuck Off, live music, craft vendors, and informational booths.

Connect With...

37 Celebrate Pride in Provincetown
42 Cruise Cape Cod on Old King's Highway

42

Cruise Cape Cod
on Old King's Highway

Day Trips • Scenic Drives

Why Go: The path that became Cape Cod's Route 6A, or the Old King's Highway, predates the founding of America and gives drivers a sense of what life on the Cape looked like before the rush of tourists, surf shops, and lobster shacks along the Cape's more bustling roadways.

Where: Route 6A runs 34 miles from the Sagamore Bridge in Bourne to the Orleans rotary. It banks north for the final 28 miles to Provincetown.

Timing: If you don't mind traffic, the peak summer travel season is the best time to visit due to the seasonality of some of the shops and restaurants along the way. But locals prefer the spring and fall shoulder seasons to avoid crowds.

While those clamoring to get to Provincetown on the Outer Cape as fast as possible might hop on the modern Route 6 to avoid stoplights, Route 6A (also known as the Old King's Highway) provides a leisurely way to get a sense of the old Cape before it became a summer vacation hotspot. The highway starts in Bourne and meanders east through historic districts of quaint Cape Cod towns. It eventually banks north, and finally ends in Provincetown. The winding drive along scenic beaches, cranberry bogs, and town centers is a great alternative to the modernized highway of nearby Route 6.

Start your drive at the **Sagamore Bridge** in Bourne, where you can enjoy beautiful views of Cape Cod Bay. Follow Old King's Highway southeast to reach the town of **Sandwich.** Historic Sandwich Village is the oldest municipality of Cape Cod and filled with antique shops and cozy bed and breakfasts. Drop by the **Sandwich Boardwalk** (103 Wood Ave., 508/888-4361, www.sandwichmass.org) for a romantic, scenic walk reminiscent of *The Notebook* over marshes to Town Neck Beach.

When you're ready, continue your drive east through the Old King's Highway Historic District to **Barnstable,** where Route 6A becomes Main Street for a small stretch. You'll pass the **Old Jail** (3365 Main St.), the oldest wooden jail in the United States, right next to the **US**

Sagamore Bridge

Cape Cod National Seashore

Sandwich Boardwalk

Coast Guard Heritage Museum (3353 Main St., 508/362-8521, www.coastguardheritage-museum.org). Sandy Neck Lighthouse is visible to the north as you continue along Old King's Highway to Orleans.

In Orleans, grab a snack or a hot chocolate at charming **Hot Chocolate Sparrow** (5 Old Colony Way, 508/240-2230, www.hotchocolatesparrow.com) or delectable donut or other baked good at the **Hole in One** (98 MA-6A, 508/255-3740, www.theholecapecod.com) before making a stop at the **Jonathan Young Windmill** (41 Old King's Hwy).

When you're back on the road, continue north. Old King's Highway merges with Route 6, to take you to Outer Cape towns. The roadway itself isn't particularly pretty in the stretch through Eastham and Wellfleet, but you can turn off for beautiful beaches like **Nauset Light Beach** (780 Ocean View Dr.) (home to the lighthouse on every Cape Cod Potato Chips bag) in Eastham.

Before you reach Wellfleet, you'll pass a turnoff for **Cape Cod National Seashore** (99 Marconi Site Rd.). Stop to stretch your legs and roam sand dunes while enjoying gorgeous

▲ Herring Cove Beach

views of crashing waves from the North Atlantic, but bring a windbreaker—even summer days can get chilly from the sea breeze.

Follow Route 6 through the town of **Wellfleet,** home of the beloved (and delicious) Wellfleet Oysters, and up through **Truro,** until Route 6A appears again. Take Route 6A (or Shore Road in this area), which hugs the coast, all the way to Provincetown's **Herring Cove Beach.** Keep an eye out for **Pilgrim Monument** (1 High Pole Hill Rd.) along the way. When you reach the beach, hop out of the car and gaze out at the crashing waves. On a clear day, you can see Plymouth across the bay from this tranquil, sandy spot.

Before you head home, take a quick dive into the Provincetown arts scene. Check out art galleries like **Adam Peck** (142 Commercial St., 508/274-8298, www.adampeckgallery.com) and **CUSP Gallery** (115 Bradford St., 323/513-3161, www.cuspgallery.com), as well as the **Provincetown Art Association and Museum** (460 Commercial St., 508/487-1750, www.paam.org). Stock up on snacks for the drive home at **Angel Foods** (467 Commercial St., 508/487-6666, www.angelfoods.com).

The roughly two-hour drive (assuming there's no summer traffic) is rolling, but nowhere near as winding as drives like the Mohawk Trail in Western Massachusetts. While there are gas stations, they typically get more expensive the further out on the Cape you get, so I recommend topping off the tank at the gas station on the mainland side of the **Sagamore Bridge.** You'll find rest stops along the route, but gas stations or cafés are likely your best bet for public bathrooms. Bring sunscreen and a hat on sunny days, and a light jacket regardless of weather to be ready for those chilly ocean breezes.

Connect With...

㊲ Celebrate Pride in Provincetown
㊶ Slurp oysters in Wellfleet

43 Head East on the Mohawk Trail

Scenic Drives • Architecture and Historic Spots • Day Trips

Why Go: Opened in late 1914, the Mohawk Trail is New England's first official scenic route. The 63-mile stretch passes through 50,000 acres of Massachusetts state parks and forests, offering a variety of seasonal attractions for year-round enjoyment.

Where: Start the Mohawk Trail near Taconic Trail State Park on the Massachusetts/New York border, a roughly three-hour drive northwest of Boston via Interstate 90 and Route 7.

Timing: Take advantage of the chance to admire the natural beauty of fall foliage on your drive by cruising the Mohawk Trail in September and October.

Few things are better than loading the car up with tasty snacks, listening to a great playlist or audiobook, and cruising down the highway, enjoying beautiful views. In Massachusetts, a simple road trip is made even better when combined with cute towns, stunning landscapes, and famous historical landmarks. The Mohawk Trail, less romantically known as Route 2, offers the perfect 63-mile stretch through Massachusetts state parks and forests to make your scenic drive dreams come true.

Start your drive on the New York state line at the edge of the Taconic Ridge State Forest in the northwestern portion of Massachusetts and head southeast. Follow the trail, briefly merging with Route 7, through the quaint towns of **Williamstown** and **North Adams** (home to the famous Massachusetts Museum of Contemporary Art) until you reach the **Golden Eagle Restaurant** (1935 Mohawk Trail, Clarksburg, 413/663-9834), an affordable restaurant right on the Mohawk Trail with gorgeous views of the Berkshires. Break for a tasty outdoor meal or whip out your journal to pen a few lines inspired by all that natural beauty splayed out before you. But don't dally: there's plenty more of the trail left to drive!

Continue east along Route 2 through the town of Florida to reach **Charlemont** and **Shelburne Falls.** (Streams and Deerfield River flank the road along the way, making it possible to add kayaking to your road trip in warmer months.) Stop in Charlemont or Shelburne Falls to

Shelburne Falls

Bridge of Flowers

hunt for souvenirs at a variety of gift shops, which feature gems from local artisans, like unique pottery, glasswork, and woodwork, as well as used books and small figurines. Don't miss Shelburne Falls' beautiful **Bridge of Flowers** (22 Water St.), a trolley bridge-turned-botanical extravaganza. (Who says infrastructure can't be a beautiful thing?)

When you're ready, hop back in the car and follow Route 2 to historic **Lexington** and **Concord.** First, stop in Concord for a literary pilgrimage. Head to **Louisa May Alcott's Orchard House** (399 Lexington Rd., 978/369-4118, www.louisamayalcott.org) and check out nearby **Walden Pond.** 15 minutes away is Lexington Common, where the American Revolutionary War started in 1775. Head to the **Lexington Common National Historic Site** (1625 Massachusetts Ave., 781/274-8300) and **Buckman Tavern** (1 Bedford St., 781/862-5598) to get a healthy dose of American history. Grab a fresh snack or a meal at **Via Lago** (1845 Massachusetts Ave., 781/861-6174, www.vialagocatering.com), with bistro fare and comfort food; or stop at **Il Casale** (1727 Massachusetts Ave., 781/538-5846, www.ilcasalelexington.com) if you're craving an upscale Italian dinner before finishing your drive.

Louisa May Alcott's Orchard House

Origins: The Mohawk Trail

While the Mohawk Trail opened as a scenic route in late 1914, its path traces back to Indigenous post-glacial people who used it as a footpath from coastal New England to points further inland like present-day New York. According to the Mohawk Trail Association, European settlers used the path to connect Boston with the English settlement of Deerfield and Dutch settlements across the border in New York. The road became more modern as Massachusetts built up its industrial reputation and, with the invention of the automobile, heavier freight needed to be transported back and forth with Boston. Today, the road is traveled more for its surrounding natural beauty than for its use as a freight corridor.

Note: The Mohawk Trail is also known for its tight turns. Observe lower speed limits when you see signs around the hairpin turn at the Whitcomb Summit in Clarksburg and other parts of the Trail. The ending to Thelma & Louise should never be reenacted in real life.

Connect With...

35 Get transcendental at Walden Pond

38 Get inspired at Mass MoCA

51 Rejuvenate in the Berkshires

44 Get your feet wet at New England's best beaches

On the Water • Day Trips • Fun for Families and Kids

Why Go: In warmer months, get out of the city and explore these sandy retreats perfect for bonfires or a quiet afternoon with a book.

Where: Provincetown beaches are a 90-minute fast ferry from downtown Boston on Boston Harbor Cruises. Crane Beach is about an hour drive north of Boston on Interstate 95 while Goose Rocks Beach in Maine is about 1.5 hours north on I-95.

Timing: July, August, and September are reliably warmer months for a New England beach trip (June can sometimes still have crisp days).

When you initially think of some of the best beaches in America, you'll likely conjure up images of the sugary sand in Florida or the gorgeous sunsets along the shores of San Diego or Santa Monica. But don't overlook New England: it has a few beach hats to throw into the sandy ring.

▲ Goose Rocks Beach

Provincetown (or Ptown) is home to **Herring Cove** and **Race Point** beaches in the Cape Cod National Seashore, which routinely rank as some of America's best in travel magazines like Travel + Leisure and online travel portals like TripAdvisor—and they're only a 90-minute fast ferry trip away from downtown Boston (plus a bike or cab ride from the Ptown ferry docks). Race Point, with its wide expanse and unobstructed views of the Atlantic Ocean, is popular with families and individuals looking for a more quiet, remote spot to sunbathe and catch some of the largest waves in the region. There aren't snack shacks at Race Point, so pack a picnic along with your typical gear like sunscreen and beach towels. Closer to town, Herring Cove offers views of Plymouth across Cape Cod Bay and has a summer café with sandwiches, salads, and standard lunch fare for those not wishing to bring their own. Note: walk far enough south down the beach, and you'll end up in the rowdier, clothing-optional stretch of sand. One other very important note: seals swim close to these beaches, which means sharks typically aren't far behind. Sharks are focused on seals rather than swimmers, but it's best to not swim off by yourself too far from shore.

The **Cape Cod Province Lands Bike Trail** is a great way to explore Herring Cove and Race Point. The roughly 8-mile loop takes bikers past sand dunes, ponds, and picturesque views of the Atlantic Ocean. If you prefer not to pedal, **Art's Dune Tours** (www.artsdunetours.com) offers a variety of tours, such as off-roading, kayaking, and sailing. Some tour packages even include a clam bake at the end.

Bonfires are allowed at both beaches if you obtain the proper permit three days in advance. Permits are limited and in-person applicants get top priority, so head to the **Province Lands Visitor's Center** (171 Race Point Rd., 508/487-1256). Stop by earlier in the day to get a spot near the head of the line. Parking is free after 5pm, and dogs are permitted if they're on a leash (you can usually take them off leash as daytime beach crowds clear out). While not explicitly allowed, I always take a few bottles of rosé to go with snacks like cheese and crackers or bonfire s'mores.

▲ Ride a bike to Herring Cove.

About 36 miles south of Provincetown in Cape Cod, the beaches of the tony town of Chatham (on the elbow portion of the Cape if you look at it like an arm) offer some classic New England summer experiences. **Chatham Lighthouse Beach** is the most walkable from town and popular for its working lighthouse (occasionally open to the public in the summer) and Atlantic Ocean views. Seals are often spotted here, too, and the water is still chilly in the warmest months of August and July (this is the North Atlantic, after all), but it's refreshing on hot days spent lying on the sand.

If you go across town to **Harding** or **Ridgevale Beach,** you'll feel like you're practically swimming in bathwater, all thanks to the fact that these sandy stretches face Nantucket Sound, where the Gulf Stream pulls up warmer waters from Florida to Cape Cod's southern side.

Ridgevale offers tidal pools perfect for swimming and kayaking. Harding Beach is popular with families, with calm waters that are great for swimming. A large parking lot at Harding Beach provides easy access for those with a car. Both beaches are a bit simple on the amenities side, so pack a bag with all the summertime essentials.

Cape Codders don't have all the beachy fun, however. **Crane Beach,** roughly an hour north of Boston in the seaside town of Ipswich, is a popular retreat for those looking to soak up some rays as well as history at the adjoining **Castle Hill,** a European-style estate built in the early 1900s by Chicago industrialist Charles T. Crane Jr. Today, it's best known for its annual Roaring Twenties Lawn Party at the end of each summer. Crane Beach gets packed in the summer with city dwellers, so plan to leave Boston early if you're making this a day trip. Nature trails, boardwalks, and salt marshes offer other activities for those wanting to do more than build a base tan. There's a $10 entrance fee for cars, and while you should bring your own standard beach gear, there is a snack bar. There are also public restrooms.

Even farther north, about 1.5 hours from downtown Boston, is **Goose Rocks Beach** in Kennebunkport, Maine. Goose Rocks Beach is the ideal spot to spend a summer afternoon reading a book between stints of strolling the shops in downtown Kennebunkport and gawking at the Bush family compound, which the late President George H.W. Bush and former President George W. Bush effectively used as the Summer White House. Like most coastal towns in New England, there's always a little friction between year-rounders and summer tourists in Kennebunkport, but don't let that get in the way of your trip. Goose Rocks is a quieter beach

Stay Off the Dunes!

New England's beaches are beautiful, but they are also vulnerable to tidal currents and climate change. Beach erosion and coastal flooding are among the region's main threats when it comes to crafting a long-term storm resiliency plan. This is why you'll see numerous "Stay Off the Dunes!" signs at area beaches, as the dunes serve as a defense against encroaching seas—and local leaders don't want to accelerate their erosion into the ocean. Tens of millions, if not billions, of dollars are needed to protect coastal towns from flooding, and beaches often act as a first line of defense. If you see hardening measures, like plantings, underway at your local beach, respect the process! It's about making sure these areas are around for future generations to enjoy for years to come.

with soft sand and gentle waves. Bring your own lunch and prepare for the dreaded parking fees ($25 per day). Restrooms are hard to come by unless you're staying in a nearby house, so plan ahead or find a secluded spot. While public alcohol consumption in Maine isn't allowed, discrete bottles of wine or cans of beer in a cooler are common.

For those venturing south of the city, Rhode Island's **Block Island,** 13 miles off the southern coast, is an adventurous day trip for anyone wanting to enjoy soaring dunes, 17 miles of coastline, or just a few cocktails from a beach club. You can catch the 30-minute **Block Island Ferry** (304 Great Island Rd., 401/783-7996, www.blockislandferry.com) from Point Judith, Rhode Island ($51 round-trip for adults, $30 for children under the age of 12). Catch the first ferry at 8am to enjoy a full day of activities.

Ballard's Beach (42 Water St., 401/466-2231, www.ballardsbi.com) is a three-minute walk from the ferry landing on the island and is a highly popular beach club with chair, cabana, and umbrella rentals, potent cocktails, and general debauchery. Just remember to make it back in time for the last ferry at 6:30pm.

Connect With...

37 Celebrate Pride in Provincetown
39 Find quintessential New England in Newburyport
46 Taste foodie paradise in Portland, Maine

45 Visit Martha's Vineyard

Weekend Getaways • Get Outside

Why Go: Martha's Vineyard has the feel of a faraway getaway—without actually being too far away. The high dunes and beaches of Aquinnah can feel more reminiscent of the West Coast than the Cape Cod shore. Oak Bluffs is a dream for any architecture buff, and there is clearly a reason why U.S. presidents like Barack Obama have made this island their summer vacation spot of choice.

Where: The Vineyard is only seven miles off the coast of Cape Cod, making it a fairly quick ferry ride from Wood's Hole compared to Nantucket. Cape Air offers daily flights from Boston while JetBlue has seasonal service. • 508/477-8600, https://www.steamshipauthority.com • 800/227-3247, https://www.capeair.com

Timing: For those like me who prefer less crowds, the shoulder season of May-June as well as September-October are perfect times to visit. But summer months are the most popular and also when all shops and restaurants are open (there are several that typically operate only between Memorial Day and Labor Day).

Of the two islands off the Cape Cod coast with a reputation for glitz, Martha's Vineyard is considered the more grounded of the two (kinda). The island has significantly greater diversity and more of an artsy vibe thanks to the town of Oak Bluffs, a hub for African American culture since the 18th century. It gained its reputation as a vacation spot for affluent African Americans due to it being the only town on the island to welcome Black tourists even before segregation was outlawed in the 1960s.

While Nantucket is fairly commutable on bike, Martha's Vineyard is about twice the size and includes six separate towns—so I highly recommend traveling by car (especially when you're trying to make the most of a weekend trip). This enables you to access everything from the quirky cafés, shops, and inns of Oak Bluffs to the luxurious seaside restaurants of Edgartown and the soaring dunes and beach walks of Aquinnah without exhausting yourself with strenuous bike rides.

The roughly 100-square-mile island is divided into "down island" and "up island" municipalities (down island towns are to the north side and up island towns to the south). The trio of

△ Gay Head cliffs at Aquinnah

△ Gay Head Light

△ harborside lunch

the down island towns of Vineyard Haven, Oak Bluffs, and Edgartown are closest to ferry ports, and up island Aquinnah, Chilmark, and West Tisbury are known more for their dune-lined beaches and rolling countryside.

In order to be closer to more restaurants, inns, and nightlife, stay in Oak Bluffs or Edgartown, both of which have robust downtown areas. Oak Bluffs can be a bit rowdier, with its bars and restaurants; while Edgartown is quieter and more the poster child for coastal New England glitz. While there aren't necessarily rows of sprawling resorts throughout the island, places like the **Summercamp Hotel** (70 Lake Ave., 508/693-6611, www.summercamphotel.com) and the **Oak Bluffs Inn** (64 Circuit Ave., 508/693-7171, www.oakbluffsinn.com) in Oak Bluffs can easily eclipse $400 per night in the peak season between Memorial Day and Labor Day. Over in quieter Edgartown, daily rates for chic inns like the **Christopher at the Edgartown Collection** (24 S. Water St., 508/627-4784, www.theedgartowncollection.com) or the **Harbor View Hotel** (131 N. Water St., 844/248-1167, www.harborviewhotel.com) can cost well north of $500—in the case of Harbor View, make that north of $1,000. Rates begin to dip in September and practically hit rock bottom ($250/night in both towns) in October and November before many inns close for the winter.

Regardless of where you decide to stay, start your exploration of the island in Oak Bluffs. The funky, Victorian architecture and rows of scrumptious restaurants and boutique shopping are an easy way to fill up a summer afternoon.

Head to Circuit Avenue, a main stretch of retail through the heart of town where you can find everything from coffee shops like **Mocha Mott's** (10 Circuit Ave., 508/696-1922, www.mochamotts.com) to fashionable finds for the whole family at **Third World Trading Co.** (52 Circuit Ave., 508/693-5550). Of course, a stop at the Vineyard Vines (56 Narragansett Ave., 508/687-9841, www.vineyardvines.com) mother ship is a must for anyone in pursuit of chinos, plaid button-down shirts, and other quintessential preppy style staples. It's probably the most on-brand Martha's Vineyard flagship store one could ever ask for. If you're feeling hungry, head a block over to **Offshore Ale Co.** (30 Kennebec Ave., 508/693-2626, www.offshoreale.com) for an extensive offering of home-brewed beer and creative bar bites like mashed potato pizzas and tuna poke.

When you're ready to explore more of the island, hop in the car and drive south on

▲ Vineyard Vines in Oak Bluffs

▲ cottages on Martha's Vineyard

Seaview Road, which turns into Beach Road about a mile before you encounter the **American Legion Memorial Bridge**—better known as the "Jaws Bridge." This (now) infamous bridge landed a spot in cinematic history in a scene that may make you think twice about hopping in a red rowboat around these parts. In real life, it's mainly a popular spot to fish or take a selfie.

Further up Beach Road is the posh town of Edgartown, which is filled with manicured lawns and palatial mansions that may seem more at home on Nantucket than in Martha's Vineyard. The shopping and dining along Main Street can skew expensive, but there are also plenty of casual spots with a view. One of my favorites is the **Seafood Shanty** (31 Dock St., Edgartown, 508/627-8622, www.theseafoodshanty.com), which has a menu full of delicious seafood dishes like the lobster quesadilla and fried clams. They also have a raw bar and fresh sushi. Once you've explored Edgartown, take the Chappy Ferry to the neighboring island of Chappaquiddick, where you can visit attractions like **Wasque Point** (11 Dike Rd.), a 200-acre nature preserve on the island's southeastern tip. Due to its location's vulnerability to brutal winds and crashing seas, no two visits to Wasque Point are the same: Sand bars shift, and strong currents constantly change the state of the swimming beach, so enjoy this area while you can!

In Martha's Vineyard's southwest corner, you'll find **Gay Head Light** in Aquinnah. The lighthouse, first constructed in 1799 and rebuilt at its current location in 1856, was the first lighthouse on the island. Located above the Gay Head clay cliffs, the lighthouse is in the island's least commercial area, with a picturesque beach (note: it's clothing optional) and gorgeous views of the Atlantic.

The easiest way to get from the mainland to Martha's Vineyard is via ferry. **The Steamship Authority** (www.steamshipauthority.com) from Wood's Hole at the southwestern end of Cape Cod is the fastest service (about an hour from port to port). Depending on the season, it arrives in Vineyard Haven or Oak Bluffs.

Before heading back to the mainland at the conclusion of your weekend getaway, head to downtown Oak Bluffs or Vineyard Haven for a farewell beer or meal. A pre-ferry dozen oysters and glass of rosé in Vineyard Haven at the scenic **Beach Road** (79 Beach Rd., 508/693-8582) overlooking Lagoon Pond is a picture-perfect end to a trip. Don't forget to collect a souvenir T-shirt at perennially popular New England staple the **Black Dog Tavern** (20 Beach St. Extension, 508/693-9223, www.theblackdog.com).

▲ Jaws Bridge

Connect With...

🟥 Celebrate Pride in Provincetown

🟥 Cruise Cape Cod's Old King's Highway

🟥 Get your feet wet at New England's best beaches

46 Taste foodie paradise
in Portland, Maine

Drink and Dine • Weekend Getaways

Why Go: These are words you only whisper when in Boston, but many argue Portland, Maine has a more innovative food scene than its bigger sister to the south.

Where: Portland, Maine is a nearly two-hour drive to the north or a two-and-a-half-hour ride on Amtrak's Downeaster service from North Station in Boston.

Timing: Spring and fall are ideal times to visit for better weather and affordable rates on hotel rooms or short-term home rentals, before summer crowds and peak pricing kick in.

When you think of reasons to visit Maine, they often include the beachside towns of Kennebunkport, Ogunquit, or Bar Harbor, or stunning Acadia National Park. But a weekend in Maine's largest city, Portland, will convince you that the best reasons to visit Maine can be found on a plate in a downtown dining room.

The number of restaurants and types of cuisines available in the smallest city to ever win *Bon Appetit*'s "Restaurant City of the Year" award may seem overwhelming. There's Roman-style pizza, buttery biscuits with homemade jam, perfectly chewy New York-style bagels, flavorful pho, Middle Eastern-inspired *labneh*, inventive cocktails, craft beers—and seafood. So. Much. Seafood. From lobster rolls to oysters and sushi to scallops, Portland's fishy offerings are endless. There are so many tasty things to try in this little city. So, where to start your foodie journey? Anywhere, really, but here are a few of my favorites.

Let's go ahead and get a big one out of the way. **Eventide Oyster Co.** (86 Middle St., 207/774-8538, www.eventideoysterco.com) is always packed; the wait for a table can go on for what seems like forever, but, yeah, the oysters are actually worth it. If you put your name down for bar seating, you can sometimes get seated faster (emphasis on "sometimes"). The lobster roll here gets gobs of praise in the press, but if you want something lighter before splurging on a decadent meal (or meals) elsewhere, just a few oysters (a dozen goes for around $24), a charcuterie board, and a glass of wine are a perfect way to go. While I'm normally a red wine

▲ oysters for sale

▲ lobster roll

kind of guy, try white, rosé, or even splurge on champagne with an Eventide meal since these all generally pair better with oysters than more full-bodied reds.

Just down the street from Eventide, the casual **Duckfat** (43 Middle St., 207/774-8080, www.duckfat.com) is another restaurant that may seem like a tourist trap based on the perpetual line to get in. But this venue's focus on, as the name suggests, duck-fat fried Belgian fries with dipping sauces or served up as poutine is mouth-watering motivation to keep your place in line. Duckfat has a full menu, with almost everything priced under $15, including interesting salads and duck-fat fried Brussels sprouts, but I suggest focusing on the fries—though maybe add a duck confit panini to round out the pigging, er, quacking out.

Fore and Commercial Street are two of Old Port's more concentrated restaurant rows and hubs for bars and nightlife. **Local 188** (685 Congress St., 207/761-7909, www.grocer188.com), about eleven blocks to the west of Eventide and the Old Port neighborhood, is a more than 20-year-old, highly popular tapas restaurant. The airy, colorful eatery is unfussy with dress

▲ appetizer at Duckfat

code and dotted by hanging plants on the inside; the tranquil vibes are perfect accompaniments to some of my favorite dishes, like the sweet potato gnocchi and local hake.

Fore Street Restaurant (288 Fore St., 207/775-2717, www.forestreet.biz), on the eastern edge of Old Port, is glitzier and known for its farm-to-table creations, featuring menu items locally sourced from fisheries or farms. The farm fare means the menu changes frequently, but I'm a fan of the Maine oysters and turnspit roasted pork loin that are usually on the menu.

Northeast from Old Port is **Izakaya Minato** (54 Washington Ave., 207/613-9939, www.izakayaminato.com), the go-to spot for Japanese small plates. The JFC, or Japanese Fried Chicken, is well worth the 15-minute walk from the center of Old Port; when you see the red front door, you'll know you've arrived.

Portland's Old Port district downtown is the hub of much of the city's weekender activities. For those making the trip into a foodie weekend getaway, the **Press Hotel** (119 Exchange St., 207/808-8800, www.thepresshotel.com) is a renovated boutique hotel in the former Portland Press Herald building. Rooms are modern with retro designs all nodding back to the property's newspaper past, and the hotel is blocks from restaurants and shops in Old Port.

Another option for travelers wanting modern flair is **Blind Tiger** (163 Danforth St., 207/879-8755, www.blindtigerportland.com), a boutique hotel housed in a historic Federal mansion between Old Port and the artsy West End. No two rooms are alike in this contemporarily furnished gem. Try to book a guest room with a fireplace in colder months or, if feeling like a splurge, reserve the Bon Viveur Suite, which accommodates four and includes a private roof deck. A light breakfast is included for all guests, but you might opt to skip it and venture out to one of the city's excellent restaurants instead.

Connect With...

39 Find quintessential New England in Newburyport

48 Take in fall foliage

49 Shop local in Portsmouth, New Hampshire

47 Sample summer in Nantucket

Weekend Getaways

Why Go: Even if preppy New England living isn't your day-to-day thing, a taste of the high-end lifestyle in Nantucket is a regional rite of passage, whether you just want to bike around the island or you happen to be in the market for a multimillion-dollar waterfront estate.

Where: The island is 30 miles off the coast of Cape Cod to the south. It is easily accessed by ferry or plane • Ferry, 508/477-8600, www.steamshipauthority.com • Cape Air, 800/227-3247, www.capeair.com • JetBlue, 800/538-2583, www.jetblue.com

Timing: It's possible to just take a day trip to Nantucket, especially if you are staying somewhere on Cape Cod, but it is worth a weekend stay to truly explore the entire island. While the summer season between Memorial Day and Labor Day is the peak (and priciest) time to visit, the spring and fall shoulder seasons offer less-crowded ferries and the chance to score the best deals in some of the local shops.

Nantucket is a quintessential part of New England history, and a go-to vacation spot for the type of person who uses "summer" as a verb. Whether arriving by fast ferry, yacht, or—like quite a few locals—private jet, all of Nantucket's welcome mats are manicured. 30 miles off the Cape Cod coast, this island is the textbook example of a one-percent playground, and it provides a great opportunity for a fancy weekend.

▲ Sankaty Head Lighthouse

Bostonians see Nantucket as the posh sibling among all of New England's leisure destinations, and for good reason. Many local CEOs, Wall Street tycoons, and politicians have homes on the island, which is known for its pristine beaches, high-end shopping, and variety of restaurants and bars downtown. The island is typically mobbed each Memorial Day weekend, the official start of peak season, for the Figawi regatta (www.figawi.com) between Hyannis on Cape Cod and Nantucket. I prefer going in the spring or fall shoulder season to avoid major crowds while still being able to get into seasonal restaurants that shut down for the winter—and snag a few off-season bargains at downtown stores—but if you want the full summer experience (which includes a higher price tag), visit Nantucket June-August.

A long weekend is the perfect amount of time to get a feel for the island and not feel rushed. Luxurious, modern inns downtown like **21 Broad** (21 Broad St., 508/228-4749, www.21broadhotel.com) or **76 Main** (76 Main St., 508/228-2533, www.76main.com) are centrally located (and include breakfast). Rates are typically under $500 per night in the peak summer travel season. Rates at larger luxury resorts like the **White Elephant** (50 Easton St., 800/445-6574, www.whiteelephantnantucket.com) and **The Wauwinet** (120 Wauwinet Rd., 800/426-8718, www.wauwinet.com), with full-service amenities like a spa or pool, can soar to over $1,000 per night on certain nights in July and August. (Note: The White Elephant Spa is a special treat even if you aren't staying at the hotel.)

Once you've picked your hotel and checked into your room, it's time to explore. Whereas Martha's Vineyard and Cape Cod have a mix of towns with varied personalities, Nantucket's charm seems like one cohesive vision, with the cobblestoned streets of downtown, quaint wood-framed and brick buildings, and picturesque cottages with perfect gardens.

A great way to get to know Nantucket is with a good old-fashioned shopping spree. In downtown, modern boutiques and high-end shops are housed in historic buildings, built from whaling and fishing industry wealth dating as far back as the 17th century. Due to a concerted effort to keep things local, you won't see many chain stores. (Ralph Lauren is an exception—probably because the brand's signature style is somewhat of an unofficial uniform on the island). Pop by **Murray's Toggery Shop** (62 Main St., 50/22-0437, www.nantucketreds.com) for an array of Nantucket Reds apparel. For regional cookbooks or a novel by a local author, head to **Nantucket Bookworks** (25 Broad St., 508/228-4000, www.nantucketbookworks.com). You can find souvenir T-shirts and sweatshirts at several downtown shops, like women-led **Annie & the Tees** (19 S Water St., 508/228-5505, www.annieandthetees.com) or **University of Nantucket Clothing Store** (14 S Water St., 508/228-4795, www.uofnantucket.com), which sells cheeky apparel like T-shirts emblazoned with "I am the Man from Nantucket..." (Ask one of your friends with a dirty sense of humor what this means).

When it's time to grab a bite to eat, Nantucket doesn't disappoint. **Keepers Restau-**

rant (5 Amelia Dr., 508/228-0009, www.keepersnantucket.com) is a bright, cheery spot for brunch with American standards like sausage buttermilk biscuits, French toast, and java from

Nantucket Coffee Roasters. **The Proprietors Bar & Table** (9 India St., 508/228-7477, www.proprietorsnantucket.com) is a funky, wood-beamed restaurant with vintage vibes that serves a super creative menu throughout the day. Brunch staples include things like a lobster and mushroom pancake with crème fraiche and caviar, tater tots rancheros, and fried chicken. The dinner menu offers a mix of small plates like fried broccoli and bigger options like chicken-fried trout. Harborside restaurants like **Cru** (1 Straight Wharf, 508/228-9278, www.crunantucket.com) are popular both for their views and scrumptious meals like sautéed fluke or seared sea scallops. The raw bar goes without saying, as the Nantucket oysters, lobster cocktail, and blue crab are fresher than fresh.

▲ Main Street in downtown Nantucket

If you're looking to get out of downtown, take advantage of the many paved bike paths throughout the island and stop by **Young's Bicycle Shop** (6 Broad St., 508/228-1151, www.youngsbicycleshop.com) for half-day or 24-hour bike rentals. If you prefer a four-wheeled self-guided tour of the island, the shop also has Jeeps and sedans for rent. For those wanting to take to the sea, **Island Boat Rental** (1 Straight Wharf, 508/325-1001, www.boatnantucket.com) rents (24 feet or smaller) boats for a day out on the harbor and surrounding waters. Those with thousands of dollars to spend and who want to really go all out for a luxury weekend can check in with the local office of **International Yacht Corp.,** or IYC, (www.iyc.com) for a yacht charter.

Off-the-beaten-path, **Cisco Brewery** (5 Bartlett Farm Rd., 508/325-5929, www.ciscobrewers.com) is about a 20-minute bike ride out of downtown and is certainly home to the most popular beer on the island, and one of the most popular in the state (save for the likes of Sam Adams and Harpoon up in Boston). It's easy to spend an entire afternoon at the sprawling brewery and beer garden in this stretch of Nantucket farmland with friends, family, and one of Cisco's popular pours of hoppy IPA.

On the island's eastern shores (about an hour by bike or 20 minutes by car from Cisco Brewery) are some popular outdoor spots like the **Sankaty Head Lighthouse** and

@Chadtucket

Despite the potential blue-blood exclusivity, Nantucket has become a social media star in recent years thanks to the @Chadtucket Instagram account—which brutally mocks the island's stereotypical "bro" culture of driving expensive cars and barking cliched lines like "Don't you know who my dad is?" (No, we don't.) That said, don't let the stuffy reputation discourage you. Nantucket is actually a beautiful spot to relax for a weekend and enjoy delicious food and views (no luxury vehicles required).

Siaconset Beach, a small historic village founded as a whaling station in the 1600s. The unincorporated town, with much of its original haphazard architecture still dotting the downtown district, had a stint as an actor's colony in the early 1900s. Today, it's a popular summer retreat with a stretch of quieter sandy beach popular with families. Also nearby is the **'Sconset Bluff Walk** (27 Bank St.), a lovely walking path around the village and surrounding cottages.

No matter how you plan to spend the weekend, don't forget to pack a windbreaker, even in warm months; it can get very windy unexpectedly on the islands. Despite Nantucket's stuffy reputation, the dress code is generally casual preppy (polo shirts, chinos, loafers, sundresses) at all venues. The island has a decent-size year-round population, so there are plenty of shops where you can pick up essentials if you forget anything at home.

Similar to Martha's Vineyard trips, the **Steamship Authority** (www.steamshipauthority.com) offers a fast ferry service between its Wood's Hole port on Cape Cod and Nantucket Harbor (Nantucket is smaller than Martha's Vineyard and only made up of one town). **Hy-Line Cruises** (www.hylinecruises.com) also operates a popular ferry from Hyannis.

Connect With...

42 Cruise Cape Cod on Old King's Highway
45 Visit Martha's Vineyard

48 Take in fall foliage

Day Trips • Scenic Drives

Why Go: Driving to see fall foliage, or "leaf peeping," brings millions of visitors each year to admire the vibrant changing colors of trees across much of New England. Why not see it for yourself?

Where: Fall foliage can be observed anywhere in New England, from the trees of Boston Common to open fields in northern Vermont. But scenic drives in New Hampshire or Maine are some of the best and most popular options for taking in fall foliage.

Timing: Leaves typically begin to change into their autumn coats of yellow, orange, and red in northern New England in September, while in areas farther south, the leaves turn a little later in the season. Most leaves have usually dropped by November, depending on when the first major frost or snow occurs.

Once you start to see the first hint of red or orange on a tree in New England, brace yourself: leaf peeping season has begun—and it's serious business. The pumpkin spice lattes flow through the streets, plaid dancing troupes frolic through town, and apple cider donuts are the only thing you'll find on local menus. Okay, I'm exaggerating—but not by much!

Plaid does tend to get a little more prevalent in the local sartorial spirit during these crisp months, and you will notice a significant spike in pumpkin-flavored anything on menus. This is also when many locals head to area farms for apple- and pumpkin-picking. And throngs of people take to the roads and head out of the city to Vermont, New Hampshire, and Maine to catch the first fall foliage of the season. If you want to join in (and you should; the foliage here can't be beat), you have several options for a lovely scenic drive.

Head two hours north of Boston on Interstate 93, to the town of Lincoln, just northeast of the White Mountains Visitor Center and home to the famed **Loon Mountain Resort** (600 Loon Mountain Rd.), as well as a variety of **cafes** and **coffee shops** along **Main St.** Grab a snack or a pumpkin-spiced hot beverage before taking the famed **Kancamagus Highway** (Note: Main St. turns into the Kancamagus Highway) east to the town of Conway, New Hampshire. This nearly 35-mile stretch of road through the White Mountains on **NH 112** has over-

covered bridge

Castle in the Clouds

White Mountains

looks and turnouts that make it easy to pull over, admire the views, take photos, and hop back in the car. My favorite stops are **Lily Pond** and the **Sugar Hill Overlook** of the **Swift River Valley.** The **Lower Falls Scenic Area** along the highway is another good stopping point to stretch your legs along its network of boardwalks. You can also take a short detour just off the highway for a classic New England **covered bridge** (Passaconaway Rd. over Swift River). The easiest way to get back to Boston from Conway is by taking NH 16 south to Interstate 95.

Closer to Boston, but also in New Hampshire, is **Lake Winnipesaukee,** which offers stunning lakeside fall foliage views, and a palatial estate nearby. Drive about 1.5 hours north from Boston on Interstate 93 to the resort town of Laconia, just off Route 3. Grab a snack or lunch at one of the cafés in town before you embark on a 75-mile loop around the state's largest lake. When you're ready to start the drive, hop back on Route 3 in Laconia and follow it along past Paugus Bay to the town of Meredith, where you'll veer right on Highway 25. Continue on Highway 25 until you reach Moultonborough. From Moultonborough head east on Route 109. When the highway splits, head slightly left on Route 171 and continue on to reach the **Castle in the Clouds** (Route 171, 455 Old Mountain Rd., Moultonborough, NH, 603/476-5900, www.castleintheclouds.org, self-guided castle tour $18 adults, $15 seniors 65 and older, $10 children 5-17, free children 4 and under). This beautiful estate was built in 1913 and owned by the late shoe mogul Tom Plant. Today it is known for its picturesque views, hiking trails, and on-site restaurant. Stroll the grounds or take a self-guided tour of the mansion before getting back on the road (Note: the estate is open late May-late October, so plan ahead).

Back track on Route 171 to the fork with Route 109. Make a sharp left to take Route 109 south, and continue on the eastern side of beautiful Lake Winnipesaukee until you reach the town of **Wolfeboro.** Make a short stop for a stroll in **Sewall Woods,** where you'll enjoy gorgeous trees and lakeside views. When you're ready, continue your drive on Route 28 to **Alton,** which is at the lake's southernmost point. From there, it's another half hour northwest on Highway 11 back to the Laconia starting point.

Maine also has a variety of picturesque towns for fall foliage, but the coastal spots are the best. For leaf peepers who really want to make a day of their autumnal scenic drive, head to seaside **Merryspring Nature Center** (30 Conway Rd., 207/235-2239, www.merryspring. org), about three and a half hours northeast of Boston. Visitors will enjoy stunning views of the

Peak Foliage

Timing for peak foliage is hard to determine. Trees can go from a bright red to completely bare in a matter of days. But in a normal year, September and October are the peak times to take in all the leafy glory. It's so popular with tourists that cruise ships are even chartered for the sake of foliage schedules.

Northern New England states like New Hampshire, Vermont, and Maine begin to see foliage pop at peak colors as early as September, while areas like Boston and Rhode Island can take until sometime in October. The good thing about living locally is that foliage shows are best experienced by residents with flexible calendars.

Watch the local weather reports and plan your trek using news services' foliage maps or even state foliage hotlines. Just remember to avoid holiday weekends like Indigenous Peoples' Day, as they tend to attract the most tourists, which means congested highways and trails.

Atlantic Ocean, while also passing through foodie mecca **Portland** and charming **Freeport** (home to L.L.Bean's headquarters). The Merryspring Nature Center is a 66-acre nature sanctuary with year-round educational programs that can enhance a foliage trip with information about the trees that are putting on such a colorful show. On your way back to Boston, be sure to stop in Portland for a tasty bite.

Lengthy scenic-drive day trips require some planning ahead. Pack snacks, water, light layers, and phone chargers. A Dunkin' Donuts app is useful, too, for any road trip, but I also highly recommend veering from New England's java giant in favor of taking a break at a local spot or two in some of the towns you drive through. Weekend traffic can be brutal on some of the foliage trails, and there's really no way around that. Don't worry about gas; most of these roads are generally in populated areas. That said, it can't hurt to fuel up in Lincoln before setting out on the Kancamagus Highway. Above all, prepare yourself to soak in all the majestic fall color!

Connect With...

46 Taste foodie paradise in Portland, Maine
51 Ski and hike in the White Mountains

49 Shop local in Portsmouth, New Hampshire

Day Trips

Why Go: Skip the outlet malls and support local shops in a charming waterfront town.

Where: Portsmouth is roughly an hour's drive north of Boston on Interstate 95. It's the northernmost city on the New Hampshire coast before you cross the border into Maine.

Timing: Warmer months are typically the best for strolling through downtown Portsmouth, but there is something idyllic about holiday shopping in the cold of December.

It's easy to pass up Portsmouth, New Hampshire, as a weekend getaway opportunity when compared to the bigger Portland, Maine, to the north or Providence, Rhode Island, to the south.

▲ Portsmouth waterfront

But this charming seaside city offers a jam-packed day trip's worth of shopping opportunities. Below are a few of my favorite places to stop, but it's also fun to just stroll along the streets and admire the many window displays in the lovely boutiques.

Market Square is basically the nucleus of any trip to Portsmouth, and the surrounding neighborhood's walkability means you should ditch your car as soon as you arrive. It can be hard to get your bearings, as every quaint storefront is appealing along the brick-paved sidewalks; Market Square is at the intersection of Daniel, Congress, Market, and Pleasant Streets (look for the towering white steeple of North Church-Portsmouth on the southwest side of this intersection).

A great place to start your shopping spree is in one of the bookstores. Part bookstore, part café, and part bar, **Portsmouth Book & Bar** (40 Pleasant St., 603/427-9197, www.bookand-bar.com) has a little something for everyone. The well-stocked used bookstore, housed in a mid-19th century building, has fairly current titles at significant discounts. Local artwork is showcased on the walls and the café and in-house bar serve up delicious coffee and tea, as well as small bites and draft beers.

Over on Congress Street is the gift shop Ten Thousand Villages (87 Congress St., #104, 603/431-2392, www.tenthousandvillages.com). Specializing in items from around the world, this fair-trade retailer is a great place to stop for unique gifts and handmade souvenirs. The shop also has a wide selection of eco-friendly low-waste home items, such as wool dryer balls from Nepal and reusable produce bags from India, as well as ethical jewelry and clothing made by appropriately compensated artisans in Peru, Colombia, and Cambodia (to name a few).

Save room in your suitcase for your trip to **Sault New England** (10 Market Sq., 603/766-9434, www.saultne.com) This popular store is a great place to shop for apparel, accessories, and home decor. The shop offers seasonal items, classic New England wardrobe staples (read: plaid, plaid, and more plaid), and bracelets and watches you didn't know you needed to round out that outfit you're considering.

As someone who aspires to the home-cook pro levels of Ina Garten or Nigella Lawson, I'm

▲ Congress Street

always hunting down local specialty food shops for ingredients to make a dish pop. **Stock + Spice** (25 Ceres St., 603/766-3388, www.stockandspice.com) is a cook's dream space, founded by local restaurateurs Evan and Denise Mallett—who also own the **Black Trumpet** (29 Ceres St., 603/431-0887, www.blacktrumpetbistro.com) restaurant next door. The shop features spices blended on the spot, whole spices to take home and grind on your own, and locally sourced ingredients like cocktail syrups and honey. There are even special house spices; the blackening rub and boom spice elevate any fish recipe, especially when served in a taco. (Stock + Spice is now owned by Paula Sullivan, who also worked with the Malletts at their restaurant.)

Over at **Earth Eagle Brewings** (175 High St., 603/502-2244, www.eartheaglebrewings.com), northwest of Stock + Spice, you can pick up cans and growlers of tasty ales, lagers, and IPAs to take home. They also sell brew kits for aspiring home brewers. And if you want to rock your Earth Eagle pride when you're in Boston, consider picking up a sweatshirt or hat. (They have accessories for four-legged fans, too.)

It's easy to work up an appetite for a treat or two while roaming the streets of one of America's oldest cities. **Annabelle's Natural Ice Cream** (49 Ceres St., 603/436-3400), just a few doors down from Stock + Spice, is popular with kids and adults alike—their pumpkin pie flavor in the fall is great for getting in the seasonal spirit. If you stroll south from here on Market Street for a block, you'll reach Congress Street, a main thoroughfare of restaurants and breweries.

The **Friendly Toast** (113 Congress St., 603/430-2154) offers all-day breakfast, lunch, and dinner in a quirky, retro dining room. The ricotta pancakes smothered in lemon curd and blueberries are a sweet start to any day, but the crab cake eggs benedict add some local seafood flare. **Café Mediterraneo** (119 Congress St., 603/427-5563) a few doors down is more of a formal (or at least business casual) tablecloth/candlelit affair with decadent seafood pastas, grilled meats, and a highly popular pork osso buco served with a peppercorn sauce on a bed of polenta.

Portsmouth is only an hour-long drive from Boston—on paper. I can't stress enough that timing is everything here, as leaving basically anytime between 3pm and 6pm can turn this into a multi-hour voyage. Make a day of it and leave before breakfast to avoid traffic. Getting out of the city in the morning isn't typically an issue, as most commuters are heading into the city. Parrot Avenue, three blocks south of Market Square, offers free 72-hour parking, but this

Portsmouth's Shipbuilding Past

Portsmouth today may be home to many shops and eateries that attract gobs of Bostonians looking for an easy day trip. But the city's industrial history is rooted more in shipbuilding than retail. Forests in surrounding New Hampshire and Maine made the coastal city an important shipbuilding hub. In fact, the first British ship built in the 13 colonies came from a Portsmouth shipyard.

After the Americans won the Revolutionary War, plans were made for various branches of the military. The Portsmouth Naval Shipyard, the U.S. Navy's oldest continuously run shipyard and technically located in Maine, opened in 1800. The early 20th century Russo-Japanese War even ended within the shipyard, thanks to a peace treaty signed here in 1905.

street parking quickly fills up. I recommend finding a garage (the Hanover Garage at 2 Hanover St. is most convenient to Market Square) for ease of access—rates are $2 per hour with a $40 maximum. Like most coastal towns, Portsmouth can get a little chilly even in the summer with oceanfront breezes, so packing a windbreaker is always a good idea, just in case.

Connect With...

39 Enjoy quintessential New England in Newburyport

48 Take in fall foliage

Combine foodie culture and the great outdoors

in Burlington, Vermont

Weekend Getaways • Get Outside

Why Go: From Lake Champlain to the Green Mountains—Burlington, Vermont, has some of the best outdoor attractions, and foodies will find plenty to dig into at the array of cafés and restaurants in its charming downtown area.

Where: Burlington is a little more than three hours northwest from Boston traveling on Interstate 93 and then Interstate 89 after Concord, New Hampshire.

Timing: The winter months are the most popular time to head to Burlington for ski lovers, but summer months are best for those hoping to go boating on Lake Champlain.

Vermont may conjure up images of maple syrup, ski slopes, and "Bernie bros"—and there are plenty of all three within state limits—but a trip to Vermont's largest city also offers a mix of natural beauty and delectable food and drink. Burlington is the perfect weekend getaway for snow bunnies or for the outdoors-lover who doesn't want to deal with packed beaches during the summer.

Church Street Marketplace District

Any trip to Burlington should start downtown in the blocks bordered by Battery Street to the west, Pearl Street to the north, South Union Street to the east, and Main Street to the south. You'll find ample street and garage parking in the area (the Marketplace Garage at 147 Cherry St. charges $2 for the first two hours and $1 for each additional half-hour). Park the car and then head out on a stroll through Burlington's highly walkable core neighborhood. The downtown area is conveniently close to everything: restaurants, shops, and highways (for those venturing out to ski or get on the water).

Foodies won't be disappointed by the excellent restaurant options in the city. Check out **Church Street Marketplace District** (2 Church St., Suite 2A, 802/863-1648, www.church-stmarketplace.com). This outdoor district between Pearl and Main streets is part community gathering place, part shopping mall, and part dining heaven. Whether you're looking for cozy breakfasts, sizzling steaks, wood-fired pizzas, or craft cocktails, you'll find it all in the Marketplace district.

Representing Burlington's famous farm-to-table culinary approach, **Hen of the Wood** (55 Cherry St., 802/540-0534, www.henofthewood.com) is known for doling out dishes like venison tartare, local mushroom toasts, and plenty of offerings featuring Vermont cheeses. **Monarch and the Milkweed** (111 St. Paul St., 802/310-7828, www.milkweedconfections. com) is a unique spot for those looking for a sweet treat with a mellow end. The confectioner infuses CBD into these edible works of art—snowmen, ornate rosebuds, and hearts (around $10 apiece) are some of the more eye-pleasing pieces. Prices generally get better with the more you buy (six for $50, twelve for $90, etc.).

For some reason, I always get a hankering for Mexican fare in the depths of winter...and **El Cortijo** (189 Bank St., 802/497-1668, www.cortijovt.com) never disappoints. Along with the standard spread of chips and dip at the beginning, tacos are a headliner on the menu. Carnitas, chorizo, and creative vegetarian options like adobo-roasted carrots offer a little something for all taste buds here.

Juniper Bar and Restaurant (41 Cherry St., 802/651-5027, www.hotelvt.com) at the highly stylish Hotel Vermont also has a major following due to its menu focused on locally raised meats and regional produce—I often save my "last supper of a Burlington trip" for Juniper's Maple Wind Farm fried chicken.

For those looking to taste some of Vermont's refreshing craft beers, there are several options in Burlington. Outside the Marketplace, **Switchback Brewing Co.** (160 Flynn Ave., 802/651-4114, www.switchbackvt.com) offers easily drinkable ales in a bright space. In warmer months, you can enjoy your drink outdoors, where the brewery also provides entertaining games. **Foam Brewers** (112 Lake St., 802/399-2511, www.foambrewers.com), near the beautiful Waterfront Park, brews tasty small batch sours and specialty IPAs in a beautiful space decorated by local artists. At **Zero Gravity Brewery** (716 Pine St., 802/497-0054, www.zerogravitybeer.com), beer fans get a variety of classic, balanced brews in a friendly, laidback atmosphere.

Outdoor recreation in Vermont is largely dependent on the weather—but there are exciting options year-round. In winter, skiing is the massive draw for visitors. Burlington offers easy access to **Stowe,** about a half-hour to the west, which is the most popular location due to the state's highest peak, **Mount Mansfield,** and the **Sugarbush Resort** (102 Forest Dr., Warren, 802/583-6300, www.sugarbush.com), about an hour to the southwest, which is another major ski resort town, and home to more than 100 ski trails across two mountains.

Closer to town, you'll find fun ways to still enjoy the winter without a full day on the slopes. **Calahan Park** (45 Locust St.) is known for its excellent sledding hills of various steepness, depending on how much of a thrill you're seeking on your toboggan. About 20 minutes east of downtown on Route 2 is the **Catamount Outdoor Family Center** (592 Gov. Chittenden Rd., Williston, 802/879-6001, www.catamountoutdoor.com). The more than 400-acre estate, built by Vermont's first governor, Thomas Chittenden, features snowshoeing trails, cross-country skiing, sledding, and fat bike trails. Equipment rentals (and lessons) are available for all activities. Rental rates vary by activity.

In warmer months, visitors have plenty of hiking options to choose from, but there's more fun to be had in Vermont besides a mountainous trek. The Lake Champlain waterfront, west and north of Burlington, has a variety of activities, from biking to boating and even nature observation. The **ECHO, Leahy Center for Lake Champlain** (1 College St., 802/864-1848, www.echovermont.org) is a science and nature museum on the waterfront perfect for travelers with children looking for a hands-on learning experience with exhibits on local wildlife. **The Spirit of Ethan Allen** (1 College St., 802/862-8300, www.soea.com) offers mealtime and scenic cruises on the lake from May to mid-October, a very cool way to explore the lake—especially during fall when you can see beautiful foliage along the water's edge. For the cardio warriors out there, the nearly eight-mile **Burlington Bike Path** winds along the waterfront and offers spectacular views of the Adirondack Mountains across the lake in New York. **Local Motion Bike Rentals** (1 Steele St. #103, 802/861-2700, www.localmotion.org) is most convenient to downtown and offers full-day traditional bike rentals for $38 for adults and $24 for children. Electric and tandem bikes are also available for higher rates: $55 for electric and $62 for tandem.

Weekend trips in summer months are also a great time to visit the **Ben & Jerry's Factory** (1281 Waterbury-Stowe Road, VT-100, Waterbury Village Historic District, 866/258-6877,

Feel the Bern: Bernie Sanders in Burlington

Burlington is often thought of as a hippie/liberal political city—and it lives up to that reputation in many ways, largely due to its famous resident Bernie Sanders. Former U.S. presidential candidate Sanders was mayor of Burlington for much of the 1980s. While Sanders, who ran as an independent, described himself as a socialist, his tenure at City Hall was also noted for an era of significant downtown revitalization as businesses began to pour into the area.

But rather than support massive real estate projects, Sanders zeroed in on improving the waterfront with a plan focused more on housing and new parks. Most in Vermont see Sanders as key in boosting Burlington's reputation as a city, so it's no surprise that you'll find many "Bernie bros" (and fans from all genders) in this neck of the woods.

www.benjerry.com) a half-hour to the east in the town of Waterbury for an ice cream factory tour.

While there are plenty of full-service ski resorts in the area, they also tend to have much higher prices in the winter. If you're looking for a weekend in downtown Burlington that focuses less on skiing and more on shops and dining, I recommend staying downtown, as these hotels (many of your typical national chains as well as boutique hotels) usually charge less than the sprawling resorts near the mountains. If you're heading up for a weekend, plan to leave Boston either on Thursday night or early Friday morning. If you can't leave early, plan on sitting in traffic Friday afternoon getting out of the city. As you might expect, pack plenty of layers and your warmest jacket that can sustain winter wind and snow.

Connect With...

48 Take in fall foliage
52 Ski and hike in the White Mountains

51 Rejuvenate in the Berkshires

Weekend Getaways • Art and Culture

Why Go: Cultural attractions, rolling terrains, quaint towns, and ultra-luxury spas combine to make the Berkshires a weekend of your choosing. This can be as nature-filled or pampered as your heart desires.

Where: Drive roughly two hours west on Interstate 90 from Boston to get to the Berkshires region.

Timing: Summer months are most popular with visitors wanting to listen to the Boston Symphony Orchestra at the Tanglewood Music Center or take advantage of some of the outdoor amenities like swimming pools at luxury resorts like Canyon Ranch. But other attractions, like the Massachusetts Museum of Contemporary Art, are open year-round.

New Yorkers and Bostonians may come to the Berkshires for the mountainous, picturesque terrain but they keep coming back for the cultural institutions and countless spas and inns in which to unwind.

It can be a little overwhelming to figure out where to set up a basecamp for a region that spans much of Western Massachusetts. I recommend starting with one of the larger towns like Stockbridge for its central location and ease of access to the Massachusetts Turnpike, or North Adams in the northwestern part of the state, with its numerous cultural attractions.

If you're in the area for an artsy experience, you're in luck. Towns like North Adams, Stockbridge, and Lenox are home to world-class artistic venues. **The Massachusetts Museum of Contemporary Art,** or Mass MoCA (1040 Mass MoCA Way, North Adams, 413/662-2111, www.massmoca.org), is a big draw for the Berkshires. The massive red-brick campus has a wide variety of exhibits, showcasing different artists and mediums.

About an hour south of Mass MoCA is the charming **Norman Rockwell Museum** (9 Glendale Rd., Stockbridge, 413/298-4100, www.nrm.org). Showcasing an extensive collection of Rockwell's famous and popular American illustration art, the 36-acre museum site, overlooking the Housatonic River Valley, hosts enthusiastic visitors year-round. The museum also has a variety of temporary exhibitions, like the Jan Brett and fantasy illustration exhibitions.

Tanglewood Music Center (297 West St., Lenox, 413/637-5180, www.tanglewood.org), the summer home to the Boston Symphony Orchestra, is a beautiful venue that offers indoor seating, as well as a sweeping lawn with speakers and screens. Pack a picnic and set up a cozy spot on the lawn to enjoy stunning landscape and music at the same time.

Culture is only part of the Berkshires equation. The region is also a health and wellness resort hub, in part due to its surrounding natural beauty and convenient access to both Boston and New York City. **Canyon Ranch Lenox** (165 Kemble St., 413/637-4100, www.canyon-ranch.com) is the most famous, known for its extensive array of treatments and programs, including "pathways," guided plans focused on specific health and wellness goals. Canyon Ranch also provides locally sourced food and four-star accommodations.

Hyatt's **Miraval Berkshires Resort & Spa** (55 Lee Rd., 413/881-1234, www.miraval-berkshires.com) is another ultra-luxury retreat known for fine dining, luxurious suites, spas,

▲ installation view of *Sol LeWitt: A Wall Drawing Retrospective* at Mass MoCA

and pools. The sprawling compound is a mix of modern and vintage, but you'll only be able to remember it in your head, not via photos—the Miraval Berkshires is a digital device-free zone. (What could be more relaxing than a weekend without being able to see if your boss is checking in?)

Yogis flock to the Berkshires for **Kripalu Center for Yoga and Health** (57 Interlaken Rd., 413/448-3152, www.kripalu.org), which bills itself as the largest yoga and holistic health retreat center in the U.S. The sprawling campus includes a forest, gardens, and access to Lake Mahkeenac, also known as the Stockbridge Bowl. Prior to its current status, Kripalu was a retreat for the Jesuit order of Catholicism (as evidenced by the church-like feel of the center's Main Hall).

Days at the Kripalu Center are jam-packed with yoga and meditation courses, but there is also plenty of time built in to the Center's itineraries for guided outdoor experiences, facial treatments, and body work. Overnight rates, which include three meals and access to classes and full use of the grounds, start at $85 for mid-week and $95 on weekends and holidays. This

▲ Housatonic River

doesn't include accommodations, which start at $110 for mid-week use of a single economy room and creep up to $595 for a double in an annex room with a view—the nicest, albeit still rather utilitarian, accommodations on the campus.

For those looking for outdoor recreation options, the Berkshires have plenty. Over at Canyon Ranch, guests have access to high rope courses, archery, cross-country skiing (in winter), tennis, squash, and racquetball. But don't feel like you must stay at a glitzy resort to get a taste of the great outdoors—the Berkshires have amazing hiking accessible to all.

The **Hoosac Range** is a favorite for those in pursuit of a hike with impeccable views (especially in fall) of the nearly 800 acres of surrounding forest. The short, 1.6-mile **Sunset Rock** path consists of stone steps and switchbacks for an easier hike than along the Hoosac Range.

The rocky, 6-mile **Spruce Hill** path affords hikers views of rock cliffs formed from glacial movement centuries ago, as well as views of the rolling terrain of Western Massachusetts.

The **Housatonic Flats** (439 Stockbridge Rd., Great Barrington) is an easy 1-mile nature walk, along the Housatonic River. It's a great opportunity for bird-watching. Keep an eye out for the Common Grackle, a velvet-textured creature with brilliant shades of turquoise and magenta, as well as various types of finches, sparrows, and warblers. The trail is also good for dogs, but watch out for the beavers, deer, and otters known to meander along the riverbank.

Connect With...

38 Get inspired at Mass MoCA

43 Head East on the Mohawk Trail

52 Hike and ski in the White Mountains

Get Outside • Weekend Getaways • Fun for Families and Kids

Why Go: New Hampshire is America's first major ski resort destination, and it remains a great place to hit the slopes outside Boston. Hikers also flock to the state for stunning summit views.

Where: Areas like Loon Mountain and Mount Washington are between 2 to 3.5 hours north of Boston on Interstate 93.

Timing: The ski season (sometimes with human-made snow) typically runs from mid-November through mid-March but can extend into April if the winter is cold enough. Hiking is more of a warmer months activity, but there are winter hikers, too.

There are many places to hit the slopes or hike a mountain in New England, but there's just something that seems more rugged about New Hampshire. I chalk it up to the state's "Live Free or Die" motto; though, really, that rugged identity is more due to its natural resources or lack thereof: dense granite deposits throughout New Hampshire makes farming here more difficult, so the state is historically more of an industrial hub along the Merrimack River and in Manchester, its largest city.

New Hampshire has long played an important role in winter sports in the U.S., with the Nansen Ski Club in the town of Berlin, founded in 1872, being the first modern ski club in America—and the popularity of the state's peaks among skiers has only grown since then. For hikers, views from Mount Washington and Mount Tripyramid are excellent rewards for strenuous treks.

Loon Mountain, in Lincoln, two hours north of Boston off Interstate 93, is a great place to hike and ski. **The Loon Mountain Resort** (60 Loon Mountain Rd., 800/229-5666, www. loonmtn.com) within the White Mountain National Forest offers fresh powder on a variety of trails for skiers of all experience levels, from beginner to expert, across the 370-acre property. The resort also provides equipment rentals as well as ski lessons.

For visitors looking to take to the forest on foot, Loon Mountain Resort offers snowshoe

skiing at The Loon Mountain Resort

cog railway train on Mount Washington

▲ view from the summit of Mount Washington

hikes (and equipment rentals) through its White Mountain National Forest trail network, with switchback trails up the neighboring Black Mountain and pathways along the Pemigewasset River. Keep an eye out for snow-covered furry friends on the trails! For beginners (or anyone who doesn't want to head off into the snow alone), the resort has guided snowshoe hikes on weekends that last anywhere from 1.5 to 3.5 hours and range from riverbank tours to treks to the peaks of Loon Mountain and neighboring ridges.

The state's most popular peak is **Mount Washington.** About 1.5 hours northwest of Lincoln on Interstate 93 and Route 3, Mount Washington is the highest point in the northeastern U.S., and an especially challenging climb due to its highly unpredictable weather and frequent gale-force winds. (Who doesn't like a challenge?) The Mount Washington Observatory scientific research lab at the summit advertises itself as "Home to the World's Worst Weather."

Note: Hiking Mount Washington in the winter is best for only highly experienced hikers. If you're in the area in the winter and you're not an expert-level hiker, check out the nearby **Omni Mount Washington Resort** (310 Mount Washington Hotel Rd., 603/278-1000, www.

omnihotels.com) for skiing, snowshoeing, and tubing at the Bretton Woods Ski Area. Like Loon Mountain, equipment rentals and ski lessons are readily available.

Summer months are the best time to climb Mount Washington, as public facilities along the trails feature food, fresh water, and restrooms. And for those who want the views without the exercise, the Mount Washington Cog Railway offers three-hour train trips to the summit (May-Oct.).

If you want to hike in warmer months outside a ski resort, drive south from Loon Mountain in Lincoln along Interstate 93 for 14 miles to exit 28 and then 10 miles on Highway 49 to reach Mount Tripyramid's Osceola Vista Campground. This is one of the state's most popular hiking destinations, with three distinct peaks, two of which are deemed "four-thousand footers" by the Appalachian Mountain Club, making them popular challenges. Given that Mount Tripyramid isn't closely linked to a resort, hikers need to come equipped with their own hiking gear and supplies.

When packing for a trip to New Hampshire, winter months call for multi-layered ski jackets and pants, gloves, hats, warm clothes for time spent off the slopes, and—if you're not renting at the resort—ski equipment and accessories. A hiking weekend in warmer months requires items like hiking boots, athletic clothes with good range of motion, a hiking backpack to store things like food and water, a first-aid kit, navigation equipment like a map and compass (cell service isn't the best on the mountains), and trekking poles. Always pack clothes that wick away moisture no matter the time of year—they are necessary base layers.

Gas stations are abundant between Boston and the mountains, and roads are generally plowed regularly throughout even the worst of snowstorms. City traffic can be heavy, so try to avoid leaving during after-work rush hours when heading north. Keep in mind: New Hampshire is the one (and only) state in the country where you won't get ticketed for not wearing your seat belt. But along the winding mountainous roads, you'll want to wear it anyway.

Connect With...

48 Take in fall foliage
50 Combine foodie culture and the great outdoors in Burlington, Vermont

PHOTO CREDITS

All photos © Cameron Sperance except: Title page photo: Rsfotography | Dreamstime.com; page 2 © (top) Gnagel | Dreamstime.com; (top middle) Jiawangkun | Dreamstime.com; (bottom middle) Ellen Callaway Photography; (bottom) Gnagel | Dreamstime.com; page 3 © (top) Time Out Market Boston; (top middle) Suchen1967 | Dreamstime.com; (Bottom middle) Wickedgood | Dreamstime.com; (bottom) Grendel's Den; page 4 © (top) Appalachianviews | Dreamstime.com; (top middle) Deb Dutcher; (bottom) Brian Samuels; page 5 © (top middle) Coleong | Dreamstime.com; (bottom middle) Realitytimes | Dreamstime.com; (bottom) Cllhnstev | Dreamstime.com; page 13 © Jorgeantonio | Dreamstime.com; page 14 © (top left) Mbastos | Dreamstime.com; (top right) Elovkoff | Dreamstime.com; page 15 © (top right) Courtesy SoWa Boston; page 16 © (top) Katseyephoto | Dreamstime.com; page 17 © (top left) Connie Miller of CB Creatives; (top middle) Eataly; (top right) Realitytimes | Dreamstime.com; page 18 © Michael Malyszko / MOS; page 19 © (top left) NPS; (top right) Lightscribe | Dreamstime.com; page 20 © (top) Jonathan Gallegos | Unsplash.com; (bottom) Rishi Barbhaya | Unsplash.com; page 21 © (top) markzhu | Dreamstime.com; page 22 © (top right) Vadim_777 | Dreamstime.com; (bottom) Douglas Mason/MassMoCA; page 23 © (top) Alpegor | Dreamstime.com; page 24 © (bottom) Sepavo | Dreamstime.com; page 25 © Aubrey Odom | Unsplash.com; page 26 © Wickedgood | Dreamstime.com; page 27 © Wickedgood | Dreamstime.com; page 30 © Jiawangkun | Dreamstime.com; page 31 © Todd Cravens | Unsplash.com; page 33 © (top left) Bennypaq1 | Dreamstime.com; (top right) Fainagur | Dreamstime.com; (bottom) markzhu | Dreamstime.com; page 34 © markzhu | Dreamstime.com; page 36 © NPS; page 37 © (top left) NPS; (top right) NPS; (bottom left) NPS /Matt Teuten; (bottom right) NPS; page 41 © (top left) Jiawangkun | Dreamstime.com; (top right) Mbastos | Dreamstime.com; (bottom) Michael Browning | Unsplash.com; page 45 © (top right) Msavoia | Dreamstime.com; page 49 © (top left) Deb Dutcher; (top right) Jacques' Cabaret; (bottom left) Jacques' Cabaret; (bottom right) Deb Dutcher; page 50 © Jacques' Cabaret; page 53 © Alexfedorov | Dreamstime.com; page 54 © (top left) Sandrafoyt | Dreamstime.com; (top right) Sandrafoyt | Dreamstime.com; (bottom) Mikey722 | Dreamstime.com; page 56 © Agladst | Dreamstime.com; page 57 © (top left) Kelly Sikkema | Unsplash.com; (top right) Kelly Sikkema | Unsplash.com; (bottom) Fainagur | Dreamstime.com; page 58 © Mimk42 | Dreamstime.com; page 61 © (top) Boston Harbor Distillery; (bottom) Boston Harbor Distillery; page 62 © Marianvejcik | Dreamstime.com; page 65 © (top left) Ellen Callaway Photography; (top right) Ellen Callaway

INDEX